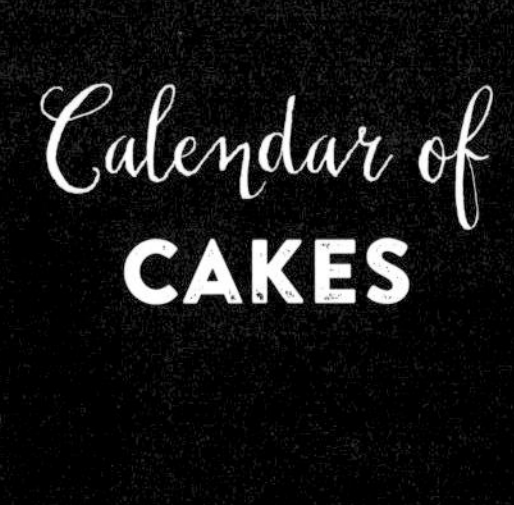

Calendar of CAKES

Wakefield Press
16 Rose Street
Mile End
South Australia 5031
www.wakefieldpress.com.au

First published 2015
Reprinted 2016

Edited by Margot Lloyd, Wakefield Press
Designed by Liz Nicholson, designBITE
Typeset by Clinton Ellicott, Wakefield Press
Printed and bound in South Korea by We SP

National Library of Australia Cataloguing-in-Publication entry

Creator:	Roberts, Fiona, 1973– , author.
Title:	Calendar of cakes: recipes, tips and tricks from the South Australian Country Women's Association / Fiona Roberts and Jacqui Way.
ISBN:	978 1 74305 383 6 (paperback).
Subjects:	Cake.
	Baking.
Other Creators/ Contributors:	Way, Jacqui, author.
	South Australian Country Women's Association.
Dewey Number:	641.8653

Calendar of CAKES

Recipes, tips and tricks from the SOUTH AUSTRALIAN COUNTRY WOMEN'S ASSOCIATION

FIONA ROBERTS AND JACQUI WAY

Wakefield Press

bottom of which has been placed a
blanched almond. Bake in a moderate
oven 20-30.
10 patty tins.
Method—
1 tsp. C. of T.
½ tsp. soda.
mod. oven 15-20 mins.

CONTENTS

FOREWORD BY LINDA BERTRAM 6

INTRODUCTION 9

A GUIDE TO PERFECT BAKING 11

BASIC CONVERSION TABLE 29

January 31

February 41

March 51

April 61

May 71

June 81

July 91

August 101

September 111

October 121

November 131

December 141

Celebration cakes 151

ACKNOWLEDGEMENTS 162

INDEX 167

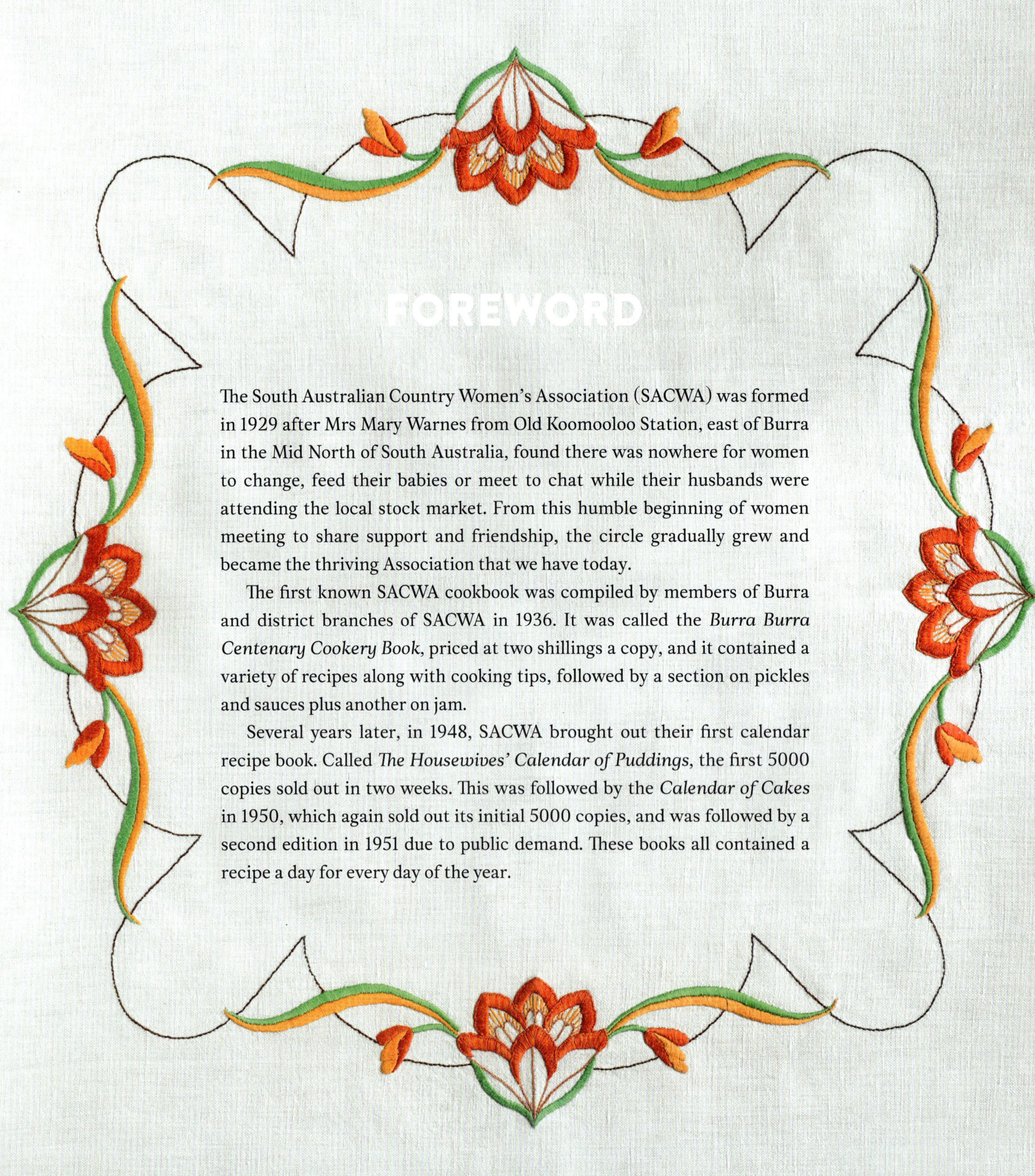

FOREWORD

The South Australian Country Women's Association (SACWA) was formed in 1929 after Mrs Mary Warnes from Old Koomooloo Station, east of Burra in the Mid North of South Australia, found there was nowhere for women to change, feed their babies or meet to chat while their husbands were attending the local stock market. From this humble beginning of women meeting to share support and friendship, the circle gradually grew and became the thriving Association that we have today.

The first known SACWA cookbook was compiled by members of Burra and district branches of SACWA in 1936. It was called the *Burra Burra Centenary Cookery Book*, priced at two shillings a copy, and it contained a variety of recipes along with cooking tips, followed by a section on pickles and sauces plus another on jam.

Several years later, in 1948, SACWA brought out their first calendar recipe book. Called *The Housewives' Calendar of Puddings*, the first 5000 copies sold out in two weeks. This was followed by the *Calendar of Cakes* in 1950, which again sold out its initial 5000 copies, and was followed by a second edition in 1951 due to public demand. These books all contained a recipe a day for every day of the year.

These were followed by the *Calendar of Meat and Fish* in 1954, due to a resolution being passed at the annual conference suggesting it would be great to help young brides and women who did not know the varied cuts of sheep, bullock, pig or calf. The book lists the common and alternative names of all cuts, with hints such as 'specific cuts of meat take longer to cook than others and are therefore more suitable for an individual recipe'.

So popular were these books that in 1960, after many requests, it was decided to compile a booklet containing recipes for pickles, sauces, jams and jellies. Over the years and various reprints the format has changed, but all of these books are still in continual demand by SACWA members and the general public.

A declining membership has been a problem for SACWA for many years, in part due to economic restraints, with many women joining the workforce and smaller country towns losing many of their essential services. This has seen a closure of some branches as younger people with families moved away for educational and employment purposes and older residents moved for access to health and other services.

Recently, there has been a renewed interest in baking and a variety of crafts, which has seen a surge in membership and even the opening of new branches. Many of these new branches meet in the evenings as this is more convenient for the many women juggling a career and a family. The need and desire to share friendship and interests is still the foundation of the Association, however.

These younger women bring with them talents and expertise in today's technology with enthusiasm for knowledge of home and craft skills using modern methods and techniques. They also have a strong desire to provide voluntary service and financial assistance for projects in their local community, as has been the objective since the Association was formed.

It's a wrap! Monique Bowley celebrating the completion of the final cake being photographed for the book.

There are also moderately priced accommodation facilities available for the general public in the inner metropolitan area at 30 Dequetteville Terrace, Kent Town, providing shared facilities or self-contained units. Holiday cottages are also available for hire at popular seaside and lake locations.

The Association today is a vibrant thriving organisation offering friendship, special interests, and the opportunity to give service to the community. It also provides a network to keep in touch with and give assistance to women across the world.

Not only will this cookbook provide valuable funding for the organisation, it will also assist the SACWA brand in reaching a wider audience outside its current membership, encouraging new members to join. This is vital for the long-term sustainability of the Association, as strong membership is required in order to keep this not-for-profit institution viable well into the future. All of the Association's proceeds and royalties from the sale of this book will go straight back into SACWA to help support women and children in communities throughout South Australia. This has been made possible by the very generous professional expertise given to SACWA in a pro-bono capacity by Fiona Roberts and Jacqui Way. Fiona as food editor has driven this project, styled all the beautiful images and drawn on her wealth of knowledge in enlightening us about key baking ingredients. Jacqui as photographer collaborated with Fiona on developing seasonal colour palates, was instrumental in creative direction and provided her specialist expertise in creating appetite appeal, resulting in these beautiful mouth-watering photographs.

Grateful acknowledgement and appreciation must also be given to Monique Bowley for writing about tools of the trade, basic preparations, cake-making methods and general baking tips in the guide to perfect baking, and to all the members of the Adelaide Branch who have dedicated time and assistance by testing cakes, typing recipes, baking for photo shoots, loaning props, following up contributors and conducting research, all of which has made this publication possible.

Put together using wisdom from the past together with expertise from the present, it is with pleasure that I present this seasonal celebration of baking, from our members' kitchens across South Australia. It is with humility and a great deal of pride and pleasure that I recommend this lovely cookbook to you all. I hope it will inspire, share knowledge and encourage readers into their kitchens.

Linda Bertram

State President

INTRODUCTION

The Adelaide Night Branch of the South Australian Country Women's Association came to life in September 2013. Two years later, it is the fastest-growing branch in the Association, attracting many younger women (some studying, many working full-time), new mothers, women who have recently retired and those just seeking new friendships.

WHY THIS BOOK?

The Adelaide Branch decided early on to undertake a fundraising project utilising some of the professional skills of branch members (in publishing, marketing, design, photography, cooking, small business ownership and administration) to create and publish a cookbook. The aim was to assist the SACWA brand in reaching a wider audience, while helping to generate revenue and increase membership.

In the spirit of what SACWA represents, this cookbook has been made possible by countless voluntary hours given by members of the Adelaide Branch. It has brought new and veteran members of the Association together, creating friendships. *Calendar of Cakes* offers a wealth of baking knowledge, helping to preserve the wisdom of the past in a contemporary way, making it approachable and accessible for future generations.

TO SHARE KNOWLEDGE

With changes in educational curriculums and many parents now working, there are whole generations coming through who are no longer receiving the valuable cooking skills from previous generations that were once taken for granted. As a result there is an increasing quest for knowledge, reliability, simplicity and authenticity to help gain these life skills.

With the increasing stresses of long working hours, busy family lives and the constant demands of electronic devices, people are retreating to their kitchens for a piece of the simple life, where they can relax, unwind and create. As a result there is a noticeable shift back to cooking from scratch at home; cooking for friends and family; being aware of the quality and provenance of ingredients; going to farmers' markets and cooking schools; as well as teaching children about food and basic cooking techniques. The recipes in this book come from members across the state, of all ages, who share a love of baking. Many are award-winning bakers and the knowledge and tips they have shared come from years of practice in the kitchen. As a result this cookbook is practical, approachable, reliable and educational, designed for home cooks.

TO CARE ABOUT THE PAST

This book is also intended to pay homage to the past by reinventing the successful and unique approach of sharing recipes, knowledge and a sense of community through the concept of a calendar. With the busy lives of today, it was decided that a recipe a week was more achievable for today's home cooks than a recipe a day.

Some of the original and highly treasured SACWA calendar cookbooks, owned by Jacqui Way's mother.

TO TAKE ACTION FOR THE FUTURE

There has been an explosion of food media in our day-to-day lives – food magazines, popular TV shows, websites, and blogs – and they are all driven by food imagery. The aim of this book is to appeal to a wide audience, including the younger generations, to enable SACWA to start reaching, educating and connecting with potential new members. SACWA is a not-for-profit organisation that relies on membership in order to evolve and grow in the future, so new members to the Association are vital.

Fiona Roberts

A GUIDE TO PERFECT BAKING

CWA cooks know that beautiful results can be achieved without the need for fancy ingredients or equipment. All of the recipes in this book are achievable in an ordinary home kitchen with a basic range of cooking utensils. There are, however, a few basic things that every good baker needs to know.

BASIC TOOLS OF THE TRADE

We're assuming you have an oven. Hopefully it will be reliable. Whether fan-forced or not, you can still get great results.

You will also need an electric mixer of some sort. A hand-held mixer is fine for beginners, or small beating jobs, but if you're a lover of baking and you can see yourself whipping up cakes every week, it might be a good idea to invest in a bench mixer.

Mixing bowls are essential. Have a collection of various shapes and sizes. Start with inexpensive stainless steel bowls; you can always add to the collection later.

A set of metric measuring cups and spoons are essential too, and you'll find it handy to have a measuring jug that has metric cup and millilitre measurements marked on it.

A set of scales is also very useful as successful baking relies on precision measurements rather than 'feel'.

Not all spoons are created equal, especially measuring spoons. All tablespoons in this book are based on Australian measures, which are different to American and United Kingdom measures. It is therefore important to make sure you are using a 20 mL capacity tablespoon. Wooden spoons can 'hold' onto smells and flavours so get yourself some fresh new ones that you use for baking only. Mark the tip of the handle – with either permanent marker or nail polish – so you know it's your baking one. You don't want to end up using your curry spoon in your butter cake mixture. Invest in a large metal spoon – either slotted or not – as these are perfect for cutting and folding cake mixtures. And rubber spatulas are invaluable for getting mixtures and icings out of bowls. If you plan on icing a lot of cakes, a small offset palate knife will make spreading a joy.

You'll be sifting a lot of flours so have a sieve or a strainer on hand.

Wire racks are perfect for cooling your cakes or biscuits.

A pastry brush is a helpful tool for lining or coating your pans and glazing your bakes.

You'll need some cake pans too. Nowadays they're available in various types of metal, ranging from cheap through to expensive. The cheaper metal pans can sometimes twist and warp, so it pays to spend a little more if you can. Also keep in mind that a lot of the newer, non-stick pans are dark. They can tend to absorb more heat, cook your cakes faster and lead to a darker, stronger crust. Some bakers prefer silver-coloured cake tins, which reflect the heat and result in a more even bake.

Spring-form pans are very handy. Use for cheesecakes, delicate cakes, and any cakes with a baked on topping, you greatly reduce the risk of damaging them when turning them out. No need to struggle; just release the clip on the tin. Silicone pans have their converts. They are great for some things but they take a bit of getting used to.

Only buy one or two cake pans to start with, that way you can assess them and buy more of the type you like.

BASIC PREPARATIONS

Once you have all your tools at hand, there are a few preparations that can aid the process of baking greatly. Then it can flow smoothly and you can actually enjoy yourself!

- **Always begin by reading the recipe all the way through.** It helps to know what lies ahead.
- **Turn the oven on to preheat** and prepare any baking tins before you start. Keep in mind that most modern ovens take between 10–20 minutes to preheat.
- **Measure out the quantities** you need of each ingredient and have them ready on the bench along with any tools needed.
- **Use the correct size tins** as this is important to get consistent results. If you use a smaller cake tin than the recipe states, the mixture will be denser and take longer to cook; conversely, if you use a larger cake tin, the mixture will be shallower and will cook more quickly.

Lining tins

- It is necessary to line most cake tins with baking paper. For rich mixtures, such as mud cakes and fruit cakes, completely lining the tins with several layers of paper can aid in a slow, even bake. However when lining a butter or sponge cake it is usually sufficient to line just the base of the tin.
- Greaseproof paper is not ideal for baking. Despite the name, it still requires greasing. It is best to use baking paper.
- You will need to grease the pan to hold the baking paper in place, but once the baking paper is in the pan it is not necessary to grease it.
- If using non-stick and silicone pans, it is still worthwhile to grease them lightly.
- Most of the time, it's best to grease the cake pan with melted butter. It may be tempting to use cooking oil spray as a shortcut, but the spray can be a bit haphazard. For the best results, brush the inside of the pan evenly with melted butter and let it stand for a minute or so.

Round tins

Stand your tin on a piece of baking paper and draw a circle around it, then cut the circle out with scissors. If you are also lining the sides, cut a piece of baking paper long enough to fit around the inside of the tin. This strip should be at least 5 cm deeper than the tin. Fold over one of the long sides of this strip by about 2 cm, creasing it firmly, then snip this piece at 2.5 cm intervals. Brush the insides of the baking tin lightly with melted butter and place the strip inside, with the cut edges flat against the base. Brush the base of the tin lightly with butter and fit the base paper into the bottom of the tin.

Square tins

Stand the tin on a piece of baking paper and draw around it. Cut out the shape with scissors. Brush the base of the tin lightly with melted butter and fit the paper into the bottom of the tin. If lining the sides, cut a piece of baking paper long enough to fit around the inside of the tin. This strip can be 2 cm deeper than the tin. Brush the insides of the tin with melted butter and fit the strip inside.

Loaf tins

Cut a piece of baking paper the length of the base of the loaf tin. Grease the tin and line it by placing the paper into the base of the tin and pressing out into the corners.

Swiss roll tins

Cut a piece of baking paper about 2.5 cm bigger on each side than the tin. Place the tin in the centre of the piece of paper and in each corner, snip the paper at an angle so that, when fitted into the tin, the paper fits neatly and closely overlaps at the corners. Lightly grease the tin with melted butter and fit the paper inside.

TEMPERATURES AND TIMING

Not all ovens are created equal

Meticulous bakers will often use an oven thermometer to check the accuracy of their temperature. In the absence of this tool, here are a few tips that can help you obtain the best results:

Oven shelves

Before you start baking, check that the oven shelves are in the right position. The shelves are harder to relocate when the oven is hot, and you don't want to let the heat escape while you're adjusting them. For small cakes, have the oven racks as near the centre as possible and for larger cakes, which take an hour or more to cook, have the racks below the centre.

Fan-forced heat

A lot of modern ovens have both the fan-forced and conventional oven mode. Using the fan can distribute heat more evenly, but it can raise the effective temperature of the oven and have a drying effect on your baking. When using the fan, it is often necessary to drop the baking temperature by 10–20 degrees.

Uneven heat

The heat in most ovens, even when the fan is used, can be slightly uneven. Rotating your cake's position halfway through baking can ensure an even bake. Some ovens develop hot spots, and turning or shifting the cake can avoid this becoming a problem. Set a timer for halfway through the baking time to remind yourself to rotate the cake.

Browning cakes

If a cake seems to be browning too quickly, placing a sheet of aluminium foil loosely on top of the cake can help deflect the heat.

CAKE-MAKING METHODS

There are a few different methods of cake making. Creaming, folding, all-in-one, and whisking. The cakes in this book cover the spectrum, from the simplest teacakes to more elaborate dessert cakes. Most of these cakes can be achieved with just a little practice and a little confidence.

Creaming

This is the most traditional method of cake making, with most butter and fruit cakes made by this method. The end texture is generally very close and fine. This is an easy method if you have an electric mixer, especially a bench mixer. A hand-held mixer works just as well, but be careful not to under-beat the mixture, as this will result in a less-than-perfect cake.

The creaming method involves beating together the butter and sugar until it is light, fluffy and the sugar is almost dissolved. It's referred to as creaming because your mixture should turn from a buttery yellow colour to a creamy, light colour that is also fluffy in texture due to the incorporation of air. Creaming properly can affect your final result so always allow at least five full minutes of beating.

If you use a benchtop mixer, it pays to stop it to lift the beaters and scrape down the sides of the bowl with a spatula.

Sometimes when adding egg to a creamed mixture, the mixture will curdle, usually due to ingredients being cold or at different temperatures. This will not affect the cake's taste but in the end, the texture will not be as it should be. If the mixture is badly curdled, the cake might be more crumbly. This is not generally something to worry about, but if you have some flour on standby, adding a tablespoon to the mixture can halt the curdling process.

The best way to incorporate flour into this mixture is by folding in your sifted dry ingredients.

Folding

The aim of folding is to achieve a light, smooth amalgamation without any vigorous beating. You want to retain the air in the cake mixture. Beating the air out of it will expand the gluten in the flour and toughen the cake.

The best tool for folding is a large metal spoon, which will cut through the mixture without squashing it.

To fold, steady the bowl on a wet cloth or rubber mat and hold with one hand. Cut the spoon through the middle of the mixture and fold it back on itself, scraping against the bottom of the bowl. Keep cutting and folding slowly and thoroughly until everything is well combined.

All-in-one

This is the simplest method of all – being just melt and mix. Mud cakes are often made this way – you'd never know that something so decadent can be so easy. The only tricky part is making sure you cook the melted ingredients to the right temperature before the eggs and dry ingredients are added.

Whisking

Mostly used for sponge cakes, this method requires a lot of aeration. The key to success is getting the air into the mixture and holding it there! Folding in the dry ingredients is where a lot of bakers come unstuck. Be gentle, and if you are having trouble using a metal spoon or a whisk, try using your hand. Spread your fingers and 'rake' through the mixture, pulling the flour up and through the egg.

KEY BAKING INGREDIENTS

Acids

There are a number of ingredients used in baking that are acidic by nature, for example chocolate, honey, molasses, lemon juice, sour cream, buttermilk, yoghurt and brown sugar. In order to produce carbon dioxide, which creates the tiny air pockets in cakes that make them rise, an alkali (e.g. bicarbonate of soda) needs to be added. This is why recipes that contain the above ingredients often include bicarbonate of soda, which needs acid and moisture to become active, but also helps neutralise the bitterness of these ingredients.

Alcohol

- The addition of alcohol, such as brandy, sherry, Galliano, rum or beer, adds depth of flavour, moistness, richness and can also help preserve cakes.
- The term 'feeding' a cake usually refers to rich fruit cakes (e.g. Christmas cake) that have either brandy or sherry in them. Simply take a skewer and press into the top of a fruit cake, creating little holes for the brandy to drain into, when spooned over. These fruit cakes taste better with age and by 'feeding' the cake with a little sherry or brandy every few weeks, it keeps the cake moist, enhances the flavour and helps preserve the cake.

Chocolate

Cocoa and chocolate produce different flavours and textures in cakes. Cocoa produces a lighter cake texture, with a rich and intense flavour. Chocolate on the other hand creates a dense, fudgy texture with a milder chocolate flavour. Cocoa powder adds structure to cakes and therefore less flour is required in these cakes. Chocolate contains more cocoa butter, which adds a silky texture to icings and ganache.

Cocoa

Natural cocoa powder is derived from the cocoa bean, which consists of cocoa solids and cocoa butter. Cocoa is ground cocoa solids, where most of the flavour comes from. Plain natural cocoa powder is unsweetened, light brown in appearance and acidic.

Dutch cocoa powder (also called dutched cocoa, alkalised cocoa or european cocoa) has been treated with an alkali (e.g. potassium), which noticeably changes the colour to a very dark brown and reduces the acidity, making the flavour softer and smoother.

Chocolate

- When melting chocolate it is very important it does not come into contact with water, as this will cause the chocolate to seize. Make sure bowl is dry and always stir with a metal spoon or rubber spatula, rather than a wooden spoon, which retains moisture.
- To avoid overheating chocolate when making ganache, which causes it to split, finely chop chocolate and place in a bowl. Bring cream to boiling point, then pour over chocolate, stirring until mixture becomes smooth.
- To add crunch, complexity and a slight bitterness to a rich chocolate cake, try adding cocoa nibs, which are roasted bits of hulled cocoa beans available in health food shops and good supermarkets.
- In the baking aisle there are a number of different cooking chocolates available to choose from, which can change the final results.

70% cocoa cooking chocolate contains a minimum of 70% cocoa solids creating a rich and intense chocolate flavour. The higher the cocoa solids content the more bitter and intense the chocolate flavour, making this chocolate a great choice for baking.

Dark cooking chocolate (also known as bittersweet chocolate) has a minimum of 35% cocoa solids, but is often up to 50% cocoa solids. The cocoa solids are blended with sugar and cocoa butter, with minimal milk solids added. This chocolate is a popular option for baking.

Milk chocolate contains a lower amount of cocoa solids, the addition of milk solids (e.g. powdered or condensed) and high amounts of sugar. This chocolate has a milder flavour, is sweeter, paler in colour and is the most popular eating chocolate.

White chocolate is made by blending cocoa butter, sugar and milk solids together.

Compound chocolate is made by blending cocoa solids, sugar, milk solids and vegetable oil instead of cocoa butter. This creates an inferior product, with a different mouth feel. It is cheaper and easier to handle, but the flavour and texture in the final result are not as good.

Dairy

- Milk helps contribute to making cakes moist, tender and golden in colour.
- If you require sour cream or buttermilk for a recipe and there is none available, simply add lemon juice to either cream or milk, as a way of improvising these two ingredients.

Milk can be bought whole or low fat. Whole milk produces better results than low-fat milk options, as the fat coats the flour particle and inhibits the gluten. Milk also contains sugar, which absorbs moisture, helps keep cakes moist and helps with the browning process (caramelisation).

Cream comes in a number of different forms and is used in different ways:

- **Sour cream** is the most common cream used in cake making, providing acidity, softening the texture and cake structure by hindering gluten development, creating a rich, dense and luscious cake. It is made from pure cream.
- **Crème fraîche** is a French style sour cream that has a higher fat content, so is richer and thicker with milder acidity than sour cream. It is made from double cream.
- **Mascarpone** is an Italian-style sour cream that is sweeter, thicker and richer in texture than crème fraîche or sour cream. Of all the sour creams, it has the highest fat content at 25%.
- **Pure cream** (also called pouring cream) has a minimum 35% milk fats. It has no additives and can be heated to boiling point, whipped and used for baking generally.
- **Double cream** has a minimum milk fat content of 48%, which makes it extra thick and very stable. This means that it can be boiled, whipped, frozen and baked.
- **Thick cream** has a minimum milk fat content of 35% and is combined with vegetable gums to help thicken and stabilise it.
- **Whipping cream** is made specifically for whipping and is ideal for topping pavlovas or as a filling for sponge cakes.
- **Cooking cream** is a light cream that has been stabilised with emulsifiers, so that it doesn't split when cooked.

Condensed milk is a thick concentrated milk that is sweetened with sugar. The unsweetened variety is often known as evaporated milk.

Cream cheese is a soft fresh cheese, often used as a base for cheesecakes and cream cheese icings.

Greek yoghurt is high in protein and lower in water content than other yoghurts, which helps keep gluten at bay. The thick, rich, smooth texture creates a moist soft cake crumb.

Ricotta cheese is an Italian soft fresh curd that is low in fat. It creates a light moist cake and is a great alternative in cheesecakes.

Dried fruit

- Dried fruit are very sweet by nature, as they are dehydrated, which concentrates the fructose. Some bakers believe dried fruit should be soaked in some form of liquid (e.g. alcohol, tea, orange juice) before being added to a cake mix, to prevent the fruit soaking up too much moisture in the cake mixture, resulting in a dry cake.
- To prevent dried fruit from falling to the bottom of the cake during baking, dust the fruit lightly in flour, which helps the mixture hold on to the fruit.
- Rich fruit cakes ripen with age as the tannins in the fruit meld together and become softer, just like a good red wine. This is why Christmas cakes and traditional wedding cakes are best made well in advance, to allow flavours to develop.

Eggs

Selecting

Throughout this book all eggs used are large, unless stated otherwise. Those lucky enough to have chooks, or to know someone who does, will know that fresh eggs produce the best cakes, due to their flavour. The best alternative is organic and free-range eggs that have the Free Range Egg and Poultry Australia, RSPCA or Australian Certified Organic accreditations.

Freshness

To test the freshness of eggs, place eggs in a bowl of water. Old ones will float, fresh ones will sink. When cracking eggs, get into the habit of cracking each egg into a ramekin before adding to the mix, in case an egg is off. This is especially important if the eggs are older.

Temperature

Eggs achieve the greatest volume when whipped if they are at room temperature, which is crucial for any cakes that rely on the whisking method to rise, rather than using a raising agent (e.g. baking powder).

Egg whites

- Fresh eggs at room temperature create more volume when beaten.
- Beat egg whites to stiff peaks before adding sugar one tablespoon at a time, to allow sugar to dissolve between each addition. This will prevent pavlovas from weeping in the oven and provide structure and support to sponge cakes.
- Fat prevents egg whites from gaining volume when whipping. It is important to use a glass or metal bowl, rather than a plastic bowl, which can scratch and hold fats. Make sure when separating eggs that no yolk gets into the whites, as this is a fat and will prevent it from gaining full volume when whisked.
- Add a tiny amount of acid (lemon juice, white vinegar or cream of tartar) to the egg whites, to help stabilise the mixture. Try rubbing the inside of the mixing bowl with the cut side of a lemon, before adding the egg whites.

Egg yolks

- Yolks provide flavour, colour and richness to cakes.
- The yolk is another form of fat and therefore helps produce a soft moist cake texture, as it helps to inhibit gluten.
- Whisk yolks with sugar until pale and mousse-like (trapping air bubbles) to help the leavening process.

Fats and oils

- Fats and oils make cakes more tender and soft, as they coat flour particles, helping to inhibit the gluten from forming, which toughens the cake mixture. Fats and oils also help preserve cakes by keeping them moist.
- Solid fats, like butter and lard, help trap air bubbles in the mixture when whisked together with sugar until light and fluffy (using the creaming method). Therefore the paler the mixture, the more air has been incorporated, assisting in raising the cake during baking, creating a light soft cake crumb. The addition of oil creates a denser cake crumb, as the liquid does not trap air bubbles as easily as a solid fat.
- When adding oil to a cake, it is important to always make sure it is fresh and not rancid before adding to the mixture. The best way to check is by smelling it. If there is a musty note, similar to the smell of crayons, rancid nuts, old butter or old flour (especially wholemeal varieties), avoid using, as the flavour and smell will affect the cake.
- When creaming butter and sugar together it's important that the butter is at room temperature, to enable the mixture to become light and fluffy. When adding eggs to this mixture they should also be at room temperature, in order to emulsify properly. If the mixture isn't warm enough, blended for long enough or if the eggs are added too quickly it is likely to curdle or split. When the flour is added, the mixture will bind together again.

Flours

- The majority of cake recipes are made using wheaten flour, which produces gluten, creating the structure and texture that holds the cake together. It helps to get into the habit of sifting all flour for cake making, to remove any impurities and help add air, making it easier to combine with other ingredients.
- Flour can be labelled as unbleached, which is slightly less processed and appears off-white in colour, as the flour oxidises naturally. Flour that has been bleached has had a bleaching agent added to it, making it bright white. This process also weakens the protein and therefore the gluten, producing a softer, paler cake.
- There are a number of different flours to choose from in the supermarket and it's important to make sure you use the right flour for the cake you're baking. Wheaten flour has different levels of protein; the more protein in the flour the higher the gluten content and therefore the stronger it is. Cakes rely on less gluten forming, to enable a soft, moist and tender texture.

Plain flour (also called all-purpose flour) is the common flour used for cakes requiring a raising agent or the whisking method, used for making sponges.

Plain wholemeal flour is made from the entire wheat kernel containing the bran and germ. It is a heavier flour, with a nutty flavour that produces a denser cake texture, as cakes with wholemeal flour don't rise as easily. To avoid this try a 50:50 mix with plain flour for optimum results.

Self-raising flour is plain flour with a raising agent (baking powder and salt) added and blended before packaging to give a consistent result. Recipes using this flour rarely need additional raising agents. If a recipe calls for self-raising flour, you can make your own using the following ratio:

Self-raising flour = 1 cup plain flour: 1 tsp baking powder: 1/4 tsp salt

Self-raising wholemeal flour is plain wholemeal flour with a raising agent (baking powder and salt) added and blended before packaging to give a consistent result.

Corn flour (also called corn starch) can be made from wheat or corn (maize) and is a very fine flour often used in gluten-free baking. It is therefore important to look at the ingredients list to make sure the flour is derived from maize or is labelled gluten free. In some parts of the world you can buy 'cake flour' which is a blend of plain flour and corn flour, creating a softer finer cake texture. For every 1 cup plain flour, substitute 2 tablespoons of the plain flour with corn flour to achieve a similar result.

Gluten-free flour is usually a blend of flours derived from different grains that do not contain gluten, for example corn, tapioca, rice, potato, chestnut, arrowroot, chickpea and soy flours. Plain and self-raising gluten-free flours are readily available in supermarkets. Grains to avoid that do contain gluten are wheat, barley, rye, spelt and triticale.

Nuts and seeds

Nuts and seeds add texture, nutrition and bite to cakes. They also offer a gluten-free alternative to flour in the form of meals, for example ground almonds and hazelnuts, which give a dense cake texture and are popular in dessert cakes. Toasted nuts provide a stronger flavour.

Raising agents

To rise, cakes require leavening of some sort, be it air, yeast or a chemical agent like bicarbonate of soda, baking powder or cream of tartar. Chemical raising agents create carbon dioxide from a combination of heat and moisture, which causes the air bubbles in the mixture to expand. There are three main chemical raising agents used in the leavening of cake mixtures:

Bicarbonate of soda needs acid and moisture to be activated and is often added to recipes that include an acidic ingredient, as it helps neutralise bitterness. It is a key ingredient in baking powder.

Cream of tartar is used as a stabiliser for beaten egg whites and whipped cream. It helps beaten egg whites hold their structure by tolerating heat when baked (e.g. meringue) and also works as an acid to activate bicarbonate of soda, when an acidic ingredient is not present. It is a key acidic ingredient in baking powder.

Baking powder is a leavening agent that assists cakes to rise. It is comprised of bicarbonate of soda, cream of tartar and salt. All it requires to activate it is moisture. Once dry ingredients containing baking powder are mixed with wet ingredients, the mixture needs to be placed in the oven promptly.

Raising agents can cause cakes to fail if:

- the cake mixture is placed in an oven not hot enough to activate the raising agent
- the cake mixture is left to sit out of the oven for a period of time before baking, as carbon dioxide bubbles will start escaping
- the raising agent has been compromised, for example bicarbonate of soda kept in the fridge to absorb odours and moisture will not work as effectively.

Spices

Spices such as cinnamon, mixed spice, nutmeg, ginger and cloves are very much associated with baking, and their aromas wafting from the oven are often attached to nostalgic memories of food. Think baked custard and nutmeg; Christmas cake and cloves; teacake and cinnamon; and gingerbread and mixed spice. Spices add flavour, personality and interest to what can often be simple plain flavours, and the trick is to balance these ingredients.

Sugars

- Sugars play a key role in cakes becoming golden, as they caramelise during the baking process. This is why the edges and tops of cakes darken, as they are in direct contact with the metal tin or the heat of the oven.
- When sugar is creamed with butter the sugar grains cut through the fat particles, creating little air pockets, which is what makes the mixture appear light and fluffy the longer it is beaten together.
- Like fats, sugars help create a soft texture in cakes, by absorbing moisture in the mixture, inhibiting the formation of gluten. Sugar's ability to absorb moisture means it assists with preserving the cake's shelf life and slows down the staling process.

White sugar (also known as granulated sugar or table sugar) does not dissolve easily, as it is a coarser grind than caster sugar. In baking it is best used as a topping on cakes and biscuits.

Raw sugar (also known as demerara sugar) is simply a less refined version of white sugar that still contains a small amount of molasses, producing a light brown appearance.

Caster sugar is a refined fine grain white sugar crystal that dissolves easily . It creates the finest cake crumb and when whisked with egg whites, yolks or butter achieves the greatest level of volume.

Icing sugar is white sugar that has been ground to a powder. It often contains an anti-caking agent (e.g. cornflour) to prevent it clumping.

Raw caster sugar is simply a less refined version of caster sugar that still contains a small amount of molasses, producing a light brown appearance.

Light and dark brown sugar are made of refined white sugar that has been re-blended with molasses to make a light or dark brown sugar. This sugar provides colour, depth of flavour and richness to cakes (e.g. fruit cakes).

Muscovado and rapadura sugar are unrefined brown sugars produced from evaporation of water in pure sugar cane juice. The result is a golden-coloured, caramel-flavoured sugar with a fine grain. It is processed at low temperatures, allowing the nutritional qualities of molasses to remain without further refinement, the addition of chemicals or anti-caking agents.

Liquid sugars

- Liquid sugars impart flavour, colour and moisture. Not all liquid sugars contain the same amount of sweetness and all contain various amounts of water, which all impact on baking outcomes.
- When measuring liquid sugars like honey, molasses, golden syrup and treacle, dip the spoon measure in hot water or spray it with oil, to help the sticky syrup slide off easily. Alternatively, place the tin or plastic bottle in a bowl of hot water, to heat the syrup up, making it easier to pour.

Honey has a high fructose content and is sweeter than sugar. It also burns faster than sugar, so cakes will colour quicker. Honey attracts water and helps keep cakes moist.

Molasses/treacle is added to cakes to give depth of flavour, colour and moistness, and is not overly sweet. It has a bitter note, like burnt caramel, and is usually added to cakes alongside sugar.

Golden syrup is concentrated sugar cane juice with a flavour similar to butterscotch.

Vanilla

Vanilla is synonymous with baking and comes in four main varieties.

Extract is a natural product, derived from vanilla beans that have been soaked in alcohol.

Essence is an artificial product designed to taste like vanilla.

Beans are cured pods that have been dried over a long period of time and have a very intense vanilla flavour. The process is very labour intensive, which is why they are so expensive.

Paste is a natural product, whereby a sugar syrup is infused with vanilla beans and the seeds of the bean are scraped into the mixture to add extra flavour intensity.

Zests

When used, citrus zests should be added to the sugar and butter mixture when creaming, as the beating process helps release oils in the zest, enhancing the final flavour of the cake.

GENERAL BAKING TIPS

- Using room-temperature ingredients is essential for good results.
- To bring butter to room temperature, take it out of the fridge a few hours before you begin to bake. If you're short on time, slice it into cubes and place it on a plate, then cover the plate with a warm bowl. You could also try microwaving it for very short bursts on a low-power setting, but watch it carefully – you don't want the butter to melt – just be soft to touch.
- You also need your eggs at room temperature. If they are fresh from the fridge, put them in a bowl with warm water from the tap. Leave them for 5–10 mins until they are back at room temperature.
- Ensuring your milk is at room temperature also means it blends into the cake mix more easily. Some also say it makes a cake lighter.
- Always bake cakes as soon as the ingredients are mixed. This is especially important for cakes that use baking powder, as the raising agent starts to work as soon as it comes into contact with moisture.
- To prevent cakes from sinking, never open the oven door during the early part of the cooking. In fact, try to avoid opening the oven door until at least half of the cooking time has elapsed.
- To test if a cake is cooked: press the centre lightly with the fingertip. A cooked cake should spring back. You can also use a thin skewer or knife and push it into the centre of the cake. If it is cooked, the skewer should come out clean. If there is any cake mixture on the skewer, the cake will require extra cooking. Give it a few more minutes in the oven before testing again.
- When a cake is cooked, it is often best to leave the cake in the tin to cool; this will allow the cake to shrink away from the sides of the tin so it's easier to remove. It will also be firmer and easier to handle.
- To remove a cake from its tin, gently run a knife around the edge of the cake tin. Turn out the cake onto a wire rack, remove any baking paper from the cake, then place it right side up on a cooling rack.
- If your cake has a light, fragile top, or if you want to avoid marking the surface, turn it out onto a wire cooling rack covered with baking paper.
- Before storing your cake ensure that it is cooled completely, otherwise mould will develop. Cakes keep best in clean, airtight tins.

BASIC CONVERSION TABLE

STANDARD LIQUID MEASURES

AUSTRALIAN MEASURING SPOONS

1 tablespoon	20 mL
1 teaspoon	5 mL
1/2 teaspoon	2.5 mL
1/4 teaspoon	1.25 mL

CUPS	METRIC	IMPERIAL
1/4 cup	60 mL	2 fl oz
1/3 cup	80 mL	3 fl oz
1/2 cup	125 mL	4 1/2 fl oz
2/3 cup	160 mL	5 1/2 fl oz
3/4 cup	180 mL	6 1/2 fl oz
1 cup	250 mL	8 3/4 fl oz
1 1/4 cups	310 mL	11 fl oz
1 1/3 cups	330 mL	11 3/4 fl oz
1 1/2 cups	375 mL	13 1/2 fl oz
1 2/3 cups	410 mL	14 1/2 fl oz
1 3/4 cups	430 mL	15 1/4 fl oz
2 cups	500 mL	17 1/2 fl oz
2 1/2 cups	625 mL	22 fl oz
3 cups	750 mL	26 1/2 fl oz
3 1/2 cups	875 mL	31 fl oz
4 cups	1 L	35 fl oz

OVEN TEMPERATURES

GAS MARK	CELSIUS °C	FAN FORCED °C	FARENHEIT °F	OVEN TEMPERATURE
1/4	110°C	90°C	225°F	Very Slow
1/2	130°C	110°C	250°F	
1	140°C	120°C	275°F	Slow
2	150°C	130°C	300°F	
	160°C	140°C	320°F	Moderately Slow
3	170°C	150°C	325°F	Moderate
4	180°C	160°C	350°F	
5	190°C	170°C	375°F	Moderately Hot
6	200°C	180°C	400°F	Hot
	210°C	190°C		
7	220°C	200°C	425°F	
8	230°C	210°C	450°F	Very Hot
9	240°C	220°C	475°F	
	250°C	230°C	500°F	

MASS WEIGHTS

METRIC	IMPERIAL	METRIC	IMPERIAL
5 g	1/4 oz	205 g	7 oz
10 g	1/2 oz	225 g	8 oz
15 g	1/2 oz	260 g	9 oz
20 g	3/4 oz	290 g	10 oz
30 g	1 oz	320 g	11 oz
55 g	2 oz	345 g	12 oz
85 g	3 oz	375 g	13 oz
110 g	4 oz	400 g	14 oz
145 g	5 oz	425 g	15 oz
170 g	6 oz	460 g	1 lb

JANUARY

New year celebrations, breezy days, balmy nights and Australia Day barbecues are what January days are all about. Stone fruits are in abundance – add peaches, apricots, plums or nectarines to the Nectarine and Coconut Cupcakes – and berry season is at its peak, making topping the Summer Berry Pavlova and Lemon and Strawberry Cheesecake so simple and delicious. To top the month off try the delightfully light Gluten-free Lamingtons, which are so good that no one will know they are made without wheaten flour.

COOK'S TIP FROM THE 1950s

Whipping egg whites

1. Add a pinch of salt to egg whites and they will whip up stiffly very quickly.
2. When beating egg whites, add a pinch of cream of tartar at half-time. This prevents the mixture from falling.
3. Eggs a few days old whip up quickest for meringues etc.

January

Summer Berry Pavlova (New Year's Day) 32

Lemon and Strawberry Cheesecake 35

Nectarine and Coconut Cupcakes 36

Gluten-free Lamingtons (Australia Day) 39

SUMMER BERRY PAVLOVA (NEW YEAR'S DAY)

This recipe is a tribute to my mother, Nell Connell, who was a renowned country cook from Moorak in the Mount Gambier district. I remember sometimes having up to 20 pavlovas prepared in the farm kitchen for local events! Over the years I have accumulated hints from various sources to include in this recipe. It is a regular choice of dessert for family functions and dinner parties as the ingredient list is simple, it can be left to cook and cool in the oven overnight, and the impact when decorated rather belies the effort involved. MARGARET PORTER – ADELAIDE BRANCH

Preparation time: 30 minutes
Cooking time: 1¾ hours
Serves: 8
Equipment: 30 cm round baking tray

Cake ingredients

- 6 free-range egg whites (from extra large 70 g eggs), at room temperature, separated
- Pinch of salt
- 1¾ cups caster sugar
- 1½ tablespoons cornflour

Topping ingredients

- 300 mL cream, whipped
- Fresh seasonal fruit (e.g. berries, cherries, passionfruit, grapes, mandarins)

Make sure your eggs are fresh and use excess yolks to make lemon curd, custard or hollandaise sauce.

Method

Preheat oven to 120°C (100°C fan-forced). Cover 30 cm round baking tray with foil and spray with oil.

Place egg whites in a high-sided narrow-based bowl. Make sure egg whites have no trace of yolks and bowls and beaters are thoroughly clean of any fat, as this will spoil the meringue.

Sprinkle salt over egg whites. Stand the mixing bowl in a large bowl of warm water. Using electric beaters, beat the egg whites on high speed until stiff peaks form, whereby the whites hold firmly in peaks on the upturned beaters. Remove the bowl from the warm water.

At high speed, beat the sugar into whites ¼ cup at a time. Move the beater through the meringue until all the sugar is dissolved and the mixture is very firm and glossy. Add the cornflour and gently fold into the mixture.

Pile the meringue into the centre of the prepared tray. Gently flatten the mixture until the sides are 5 cm high. Use the point of a spoon to scoop the sides up from the tray to create decorative edges. Avoid creating points of meringue, as these could burn. Spread the mixture from the centre to the edges to increase the diameter of the pavlova.

Reduce the oven temperature to 110°C (90°C fan-forced) and bake for 1½ hours. Turn off oven and allow the pavlova to cool in the oven.

Once cooled, cover the pavlova with baking paper and a light tray, invert (turn upside down). Gently remove the foil. Place a serving plate over the base of the pavlova and gently turn back over.

Decorate with whipped cream and fresh summer fruits.

LEMON AND STRAWBERRY CHEESECAKE

The origin of the recipe is unknown other than it has always been a family favourite, firstly made by my now 93-year-old grandmother, then my mum and now me. I was 'handed over' the recipe at my kitchen tea, prior to my wedding, by my mum when family and friends were invited to share a recipe in lieu of gifts. Over the years it has proven to be a great success! The lemon cheesecake is always requested at birthdays, parties and other family events. I simply change the decoration on top to suit the occasion (a sprinkle of nutmeg, some strawberries, a Peppa Pig figurine, footballs, etc.). Even those that are not fans of cheesecake say this is 'the best cheesecake ever!'. TRACY SMITH – ADELAIDE BRANCH

Preparation time: 30 minutes
Cooking time: 15 minutes
Serves: 10–12
Equipment: 24 cm springform pan

Ingredients
250 g packet Nice biscuits
125 g unsalted butter, melted
400 g tin condensed milk
250 g packet cream cheese, softened
1 large free-range egg, separated
1/4 cup (60 mL) lemon juice
Zest of 1 lemon
1 punnet strawberries, hulled and sliced

Method
Preheat oven to 140°C (120°C fan-forced) and line the base of a 24 cm springform tin with baking paper.

Using a rolling pin, crush the biscuits between two sheets of baking paper until they resemble fine crumbs. Alternatively, place biscuits in a food processor and pulse to a fine crumb. Place in a medium mixing bowl, add melted butter and mix with a spoon until combined. Press the biscuit mixture into the base of the prepared springform tin and refrigerate for 1 hour or until firm.

In a mixing bowl, add condensed milk, cream cheese and egg yolk, stirring until smooth and well combined. Add lemon juice and zest and stir until well combined.

In a separate bowl beat the egg white with electric beaters until stiff peaks form. Using a large metal spoon, gently fold egg whites into cheese mixture until just combined.

Pour the filling over the chilled biscuit base and bake in preheated oven for approximately 15 minutes or until cooked through. Remove from oven and allow to cool, before decorating with fresh strawberries or summer fruit (e.g. mixed berries, passionfruit, stone fruit, mango).

Tip

To cut perfect slices of cheesecake, use a sharp cook's knife dipped in hot water.

NECTARINE AND COCONUT CUPCAKES

I grew up on a farm with wheat, grain, cattle, sheep, pigs, chooks – the lot. Mum would make this cake using home-churned butter, fresh eggs and milk, and serve it warm. It would be gone in a flash! I've been making it for almost 50 years too. While the men are out harvesting, I'll make it for their afternoon tea. It's versatile – you can use nectarines, apricots, peaches, plums, cherries and grapes, and I'll sometimes improvise with sultanas on top or make it with a macaroon or streusel topping.

GLENDA NOAK – CADELL MORGAN BRANCH

Preparation time: 30 minutes
Cooking time: 30 minutes
Serves: 12 cupcakes
Equipment: 1 x 12-hole standard muffin pan or 2 x 20 cm square cake tins

Cake ingredients

2 cups self-raising flour
Pinch of salt
1/2 cup sugar
1/2 cup (125 mL) milk
1 large free-range egg, lightly beaten
1 1/2 tablespoons unsalted butter, melted
1/2 teaspoon finely grated lemon zest
400 g nectarines, halved, de-stoned and sliced, or any other seasonal fruit (e.g. peaches, apricots, plums, cherries, grapes)

Topping ingredients

80 g softened butter
1/2 cup sugar
1 egg, lightly beaten
1 1/2 cups shredded coconut

Method

Preheat oven to 180°C (160°C fan-forced) and lightly grease 1 x 12-hole standard muffin pans or 2 x 20 cm square cake tins and line with baking paper or muffin cases.

Place the flour, salt, sugar, milk, egg, butter and zest together in a large mixing bowl, stirring until well combined. Spoon the mixture into the prepared tins and flatten out with slightly more mix at the corners of each tin.

Place a layer of the sliced or halved fruit (face up) over the top and gently press the fruit into the mix.

For the topping, place the butter and sugar together in a small mixing bowl and using electric beaters beat together until light and fluffy. Add the egg and beat until combined. Finally add the shredded coconut and gently stir until well combined. Sprinkle the topping over the fruit, place cake tins in preheated oven for 30 minutes for large cakes and 20 minutes for cupcakes or until a skewer comes out clean.

Tip

For an alternative streusel topping rub together 1 1/2 cups of plain flour, 1/2 cup sugar, teaspoon vanilla essence, pinch of cinnamon and 90 g softened butter together to a breadcrumb consistency and sprinkle over fruit topping.

GLUTEN-FREE LAMINGTONS (AUSTRALIA DAY)

It's great to have sweet treats that taste normal but are gluten free, and lamingtons are no exception! I think we should all be able to enjoy this traditional Australian treat. This recipe is my own and I've been making it for almost a decade. They are always such a hit at parties and on Australia Day everyone always says, 'More please!'. PAMELA MORIARTY – ADELAIDE BRANCH

Preparation time: 20 minutes

Cooking time: 20 minutes

Serves: 12

Equipment: 20 cm square tin

Cake ingredients

- 2 large free-range eggs, lightly beaten
- 1/3 cup caster sugar
- 1/4 cup tapioca flour
- 1/4 cup pure (maize) cornflour
- 1 tablespoon gluten-free self-raising flour
- 1/2 teaspoon gluten-free baking powder
- 1 tablespoon unsalted butter, melted
- 1 tablespoon boiling water

Icing ingredients

- 2 cups pure icing sugar, sifted
- 1/3 cup unsweetened Dutch cocoa, sifted
- 1/2 cup (125 mL) boiling water
- 1 tablespoon unsalted butter
- 1 cup shredded or desiccated coconut

Method

Preheat oven to 180°C (160°C fan-forced) and lightly grease and line a 20 cm square tin with baking paper.

Beat eggs and caster sugar in the small bowl of an electric mixer on the highest speed setting for 5 minutes, or until mixture becomes thick and glossy.

Combine flours and baking powder together and sift twice.

Add flour mixture a few spoonfuls at a time into egg mixture, folding gently using a large metal spoon, until just combined. Add melted butter and boiling water, stirring until just combined. Do not over-stir.

Pour mixture into prepared tin and bake for approximately 20 minutes or until sponge springs back when lightly pressed in the centre. Cool sponge in tin for 5 minutes before turning onto on a wire rack, to cool completely.

Cut sponge into 12 equal portions and wait until firm (or freeze for 30 minutes – see cook's tip) before icing.

Meanwhile to make the icing, combine icing sugar, cocoa, boiling water and butter, stirring until mixture becomes smooth. Dip sponge into icing and roll in coconut. Place the lamingtons on a wire rack to set. Store in an airtight container.

Tip

Lamingtons are traditionally made with day-old sponge. To make lamingtons on the day you've baked them pop the cooled sponge portions into the freezer to firm up before coating in icing and coconut

FEBRUARY

Summer days call for fresh seasonal flavours, like peaches, blueberries and raspberries all begging to be baked. From 'Free' Blueberry and Banana Bread, perfect toasted for brunch, to a delicious vegan Peach Melba Buckle Cake that is hard to believe has no eggs, these flavours are irresistible. At the more sinful end of the scale, try the Raspberry Belgian Bun, perfect for any homemade berry jam, or the decadent Chocolate and Berry Roulade to share with your Valentine.

COOK'S TIP FROM THE 1950s

Oven reminder

If you have a cake in the oven that you may forget, place a piece of paper in the oven door when closing it, so that most of it sticks out. Alternately, spear a piece on the door handle. This will draw your attention every time you go near the stove.

February

'Free' Blueberry and Banana Bread 43

Chocolate and Berry Roulade (Valentine's Day) 44

Raspberry Belgian Bun 47

Peach Melba Buckle Cake.. 48

'FREE' BLUEBERRY AND BANANA BREAD

One of my favourite things to bake and guiltlessly eat is my gluten, dairy and sugar free banana and blueberry bread. While I generally stick to baking a rotation of foods that are fairly high in butter and sugar, I love that this recipe's fruit, honey, nuts and eggs make it just as good for a breakfast treat when served with ricotta and berries as it does a tasty dessert with a berry coulis and double cream. I should probably mention that this recipe has reached 'edible paper' status in my recipe file.

MIM GOLLAN – ADELAIDE BRANCH

Method

Preheat oven to 160°C (140°C fan-forced) and lightly grease a 1.5 litre loaf tin or 12 x 1/2 cup capacity mini loaf tins.

In a blender combine the banana, egg, honey, vanilla, olive oil, bicarbonate of soda and lemon juice. Blitz until smooth.

Transfer the banana mixture into a large mixing bowl and fold through the almond meal, flaxseed meal and blueberries.

If using one large tin, spoon the batter into the prepared tin and bake for 45 minutes to 1 hour or until a skewer comes out dry. If the loaf is over-browning but uncooked, cover with brown paper or foil, to prevent the top colouring further. Allow loaf to cool in tin, before turning out.

I also like to make these as 12 individual small cakes, which are great to keep on standby in the freezer. Bake in preheated oven for 20–25 minutes or until a skewer comes out of the centre clean.

Preparation time: 20 minutes
Cooking time: 1 hour for the large tin or 25 minutes for individual tins
Serves: 12
Equipment: 1.5 litre loaf tin or 12 x 1/2 cup mini loaf tins

Ingredients

- 400 g ripe peeled bananas
- 4 large free-range eggs
- 1/4 cup honey
- 1 teaspoon vanilla
- 1/3 cup (80 mL) olive oil
- 1/2 teaspoon ground cinnamon
- 1 teaspoon bicarbonate of soda
- 1 tablespoon lemon juice
- 2 1/4 cups almond meal
- 1/3 cup flaxseed meal
- 125 g blueberries

This cake works just as well with hazelnut meal, and if blueberries are not available add raspberries, blackberries or chopped strawberries.

CHOCOLATE AND BERRY ROULADE (VALENTINE'S DAY)

This is a recipe adapted from one by Margaret Kirkwood. She was a trailblazer in cooking in South Australia, and was one of the first TV, radio and print cooking personalities. She was an original MasterChef, I suppose! In the 70s, Mum did classes with her in her cooking school. She's been making this cake since then – it has become the family's special occasion cake. Initially it was at the children's insistence but even now, as grown adults, it still appears for birthdays. People are usually very complimentary – Mum's had a few proclaiming it's the best they've ever tasted. She says it's almost embarrassing as it's a very simple cake to make. JACQUI WAY – ADELAIDE BRANCH

Preparation time: 20 minutes
Cooking time: 15–20 minutes
Serves: 8
Cake tin size: 32 cm x 24 cm Swiss roll pan

Cake ingredients

- 5 large free-range eggs, separated
- 1 cup caster sugar
- 170 g dark chocolate, melted and cooled slightly

Filling ingredients

- Icing sugar, to dust
- 300 mL thickened cream, whipped
- 30 g dark chocolate, melted
- 1 punnet raspberries or strawberries

Method

Preheat oven to 180°C (160°C fan-forced) and lightly grease a 32 cm x 24 cm Swiss roll pan and line with enough baking paper to come up the sides of the pan.

Place the egg yolks and sugar together in a large mixing bowl and beat until pale and creamy. Add the melted chocolate, gently stirring to combine. In a separate bowl beat egg whites to stiff peaks and gently fold into chocolate mixture until combined. Spread chocolate mixture on prepared Swiss roll tin and place in preheated oven for 15–20 minutes, or until the top is firm and hollow sounding. Remove from oven and cover cake with a damp cloth or tea towel.

Leave cake covered overnight or until it has cooled and the top is soft. Dust the cake generously with icing sugar. Take a fresh piece of baking paper, slightly longer than the Swiss roll tin, and place over the top of cake, carefully turning the cake over. Remove original paper case and spread underside of cake with half the whipped cream, reserving the remainder for the top.

Meanwhile spread the melted chocolate on baking paper, allowing it to set, then break into shards. Carefully roll the cake up and decorate the top with chocolate shards, cream and berries.

This is also great as a Christmas Yule log, dusted with icing sugar and decorated with holly.

RASPBERRY BELGIAN BUN

My mother made this every week for about 60 years – right up until she was in her late 70s. My dad loved it, and it was always there in a tin for him when he came home at night. I've been making it since I was about 14 years old, so it's part and parcel with what I remember from my childhood and what I remember of my mother. I've passed it on to my own daughter-in-law who makes it now too, so it will live on. It keeps quite well, and it seems to have more flavour the day after it's made, but it usually never lasts that long. It's such a simple recipe but it's just got that something about it. Isn't that the way? You usually find the simple things are the best. YVONNE MEDLEN – TEA TREE GULLY BRANCH

Preparation time: 30 minutes

Cooking time: 20 minutes

Serves: 8

Equipment: 20 cm sandwich tin

Ingredients

- 125 g unsalted butter, softened
- 125 g caster sugar
- 1 egg, lightly beaten
- 125 g plain flour, sifted
- 125 g self-raising flour, sifted
- Pinch of salt
- 1/2 cup raspberry jam
- 1/2 cup blanched almonds, halved

Method

Preheat oven to 170°C (150°C fan-forced) and line a 20 cm sandwich tin with baking paper.

Combine butter and sugar in a large mixing bowl and beat with electric beaters until the mixture is light and fluffy. Add egg, beating until combined.

Add the sifted flours and salt to the butter mixture, stirring to combine, until mixture comes together as a soft dough.

Divide the dough into two equal pieces, pressing one half evenly into the base of the prepared sandwich tin. Evenly spread the raspberry jam over the top. Press the remaining dough over the jam, taking it to the edge of the tin. Sprinkle the blanched almonds over the top.

Place tin in preheated oven for 25–30 minutes, or until top is golden brown. Remove from oven and allow to cool.

This cake keeps very well and is best served in slices.

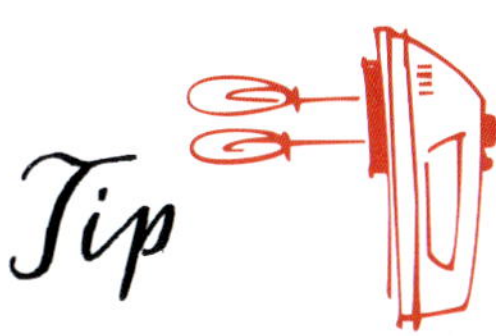

Tip

Always use butter as it doesn't taste the same with margarine. Put as many blanched almonds on top as you can.

PEACH MELBA BUCKLE CAKE

This is a summertime favourite and a fantastic way to make the most of that stone fruit that might have got a bit bruised on the way home from the markets. It's a great cake to take to a lunch or afternoon tea – it looks pretty, is not too heavy or rich for a warm day and it's super delicious. The almond and spices compliment the peaches beautifully. This is a recipe that I've adapted to make dairy-free and vegan-friendly, but no one can ever believe it's a vegan cake. PIXIE STARDUST – ADELAIDE BRANCH

Preparation time: 10 minutes
Cooking time: 50 minutes
Serves: 8
Equipment: 20 cm round cake tin

Cake ingredients
2/3 cup almond meal
1 1/2 cups plain flour
2 teaspoons baking powder
1/2 teaspoon bicarbonate of soda
1/2 teaspoon salt
1/2 teaspoon ground cinnamon
1/2 teaspoon ground cardamom
1/4 teaspoon grated nutmeg
1 cup (250 mL) almond milk
2 teaspoons apple cider vinegar
2/3 cup caster sugar
1/3 cup (80 mL) sunflower oil
2 teaspoons pure vanilla extract

Topping ingredients
4 peaches, de-stoned and sliced
1/2 punnet raspberries
1 tablespoon demerara or brown sugar
1/2 teaspoon ground cinnamon

Method

Preheat oven to 180°C (160°C fan-forced) and lightly grease and line a 20 cm round cake tin with baking paper.

In a large bowl mix the almond meal, flour, baking powder, bicarbonate of soda, salt, cinnamon, cardamom and nutmeg together, stirring until well combined.

In a second bowl whisk the almond milk and vinegar together, allowing it to sit for a few minutes. Add the sugar, oil and vanilla to the milk mixture, whisking to combine.

Pour the wet mixture into the dry mixture, stirring gently to combine. Pour cake mixture into the prepared cake tin.

Meanwhile, for the topping, place peach slices, raspberries, sugar and cinnamon together in a mixing bowl, tossing until well coated. Arrange the peach slices and raspberries on top of the cake mixture and sprinkle over any leftover cinnamon sugar.

Place tin in preheated oven for 50 minutes or until a skewer inserted into the centre comes out with a few moist crumbs. Allow to cool for 20 minutes before serving.

This can also be made with other stone fruit or a combination of stone fruit and fresh berries.

Using spelt flour instead of plain flour gives a nice flavour and texture to the cake. Let the almond milk and vinegar sit for a bit to curdle and to help it react better with the bicarbonate of soda.

MARCH

The days are getting shorter and leaves are turning, creating a patchwork of colour for Sunday drives. Crisp new season apples are ready for picking, perfect in the Apple, Walnut and Cinnamon Teacake, made with the SACWA Scone Mix. Juicy fresh figs are in abundance and partner beautifully with walnuts and goats cheese, show-cased in the modern version of the Walnut and Fig Torte, made with a cream or goats curd cheese frosting. The last of the season's plums are begging to be eaten and if you're a fan of fruit crumbles then the Plum Streusel Cake is the one for you. If fruit cake is your weakness, try the delicious rich Irish Porter Cake, made with Irish stout and traditionally served on St Patrick's Day.

COOK'S TIP FROM THE 1950s

Turning out sandwich cakes

If sponges or sandwich cakes appear to be sticking to the tins, wipe over the bottom of tins with a wet, cold cloth, or alternately, stand tins for a minute on a wet cloth. The sponge will then come away quite clean, with edges intact.

March

Walnut and Fig Torte.....52

Apple, Walnut and Cinnamon Teacake.....55

Irish Porter Cake (St Patrick's Day).....56

Plum Streusel Cake.....59

WALNUT AND FIG TORTE

In 1975 I was living with my sister in Adelaide and studying a night class in floral art. At the class I met a friendly police lady who I invited to have tea with my sister and I. She brought this cake over for tea and we enjoyed it so much we asked her for the recipe. I have been making it ever since, mainly for family birthdays. It is very popular with my family as it is nice and a bit different. I always get people to try and guess the ingredients of the cake and no one ever guesses it has SAO biscuits in it.

YAE SCHOENHENZEL – LOXTON DISTRICT

Preparation time: 20 minutes
Cooking time: 30 minutes
Serves: 8–10
Equipment: 20 cm springform cake tin or 1 litre capacity loaf tin

Cake ingredients

- 3 large free-range egg whites
- 1 cup sugar
- ½–¾ cup walnuts, roughly chopped
- 1 teaspoon baking powder
- 14 SAO biscuits, crushed to a fine crumb

Topping ingredients

- 300 mL thickened cream, whipped
- 50g dark chocolate, grated or curled
- 3 fresh figs, quartered

Method

Preheat oven to 180°C (160°C fan-forced) and lightly grease and line a 20 cm round springform tin or 1 litre capacity loaf tin with baking paper.

Place egg whites in a medium mixing bowl and using an electric beater whisk until the mixture holds its shape. Gradually add the sugar, 1 tablespoon at a time, beating continuously between additions to make sure sugar is dissolved. Add walnuts, baking powder and biscuit crumbs to the mixture, folding gently until combined.

Spoon mixture into prepared cake tin and place in preheated oven for 30 minutes.

When the cake has cooled, remove from tin and carefully remove baking paper from the base. Halve cake and spread whipped cream through the centre and on top. Place figs on top and sprinkle with chocolate curls, using a peeler.

An alternative topping for something a little different is to place 250 g softened cream cheese, 200 g goats curd and ¼ cup icing sugar together in a mixing bowl and beat until smooth. This combination goes beautifully with the walnuts, figs and chocolate.

Tip

If you haven't got a food processor you can put the biscuits in a bag and hit it with a rolling pin to break them up.

APPLE, WALNUT AND CINNAMON TEACAKE

I created this recipe several years ago for a Laucke scone mix competition. I needed to come up with a sweet or savoury recipe using the Laucke scone mix and this is what I came up with. I won the competition and my recipe is on the Laucke website and will be printed on the box at some stage. When I was testing this recipe I took it along to my sewing group who suggested I add more apple. Then I took it to my CWA branch and they suggested I add more cinnamon. I tweaked the recipe a little more and then entered the competition. Now I like to make it for afternoon tea and then I have the leftovers for dessert with some warm custard. My husband grows all kinds of apples as a hobby and I like trying this with different kinds. LYNETTE BREW – TANUNDA BRANCH

Preparation time: 20 minutes
Cooking time: 30 minutes
Serves: 16 or 2 x loaves for 8
Cake tin size: 2 x 24 cm x 7 cm loaf tin

Ingredients

- 600 g pack Laucke SACWA scone mix
- 280 mL water
- 1 tablespoon ground cinnamon
- 2 teaspoons vanilla essence
- 2 medium apples, grated
- 2/3 cup walnuts, chopped
- 2 tablespoons sugar
- 2 tablespoons (40 mL) melted unsalted butter

Method

Preheat oven to 200°C (180°C fan-forced) and lightly grease and line 2 x 24 cm x 7 cm loaf tins with baking paper.

Place the scone mix in a large mixing bowl with water, half the cinnamon and vanilla, mixing until well combined. Knead the dough until soft, smooth and sticky and you will be rewarded with a soft, moist loaf that will stay fresh for longer. This is easily achieved using an electric mixer with a dough hook, at medium speed.

Add the grated apple and half the nuts and mix until combined. The dough is quite sticky to work with, so it helps to dust hands with flour, but don't add extra flour to the mix. Once the dough comes together, allow to rest for 5 minutes. Divide into two equal portions and place in prepared tins. Gently press the remaining nuts on top and allow to rest for a further 5 minutes.

Place tins in preheated oven for 30 minutes or until a skewer comes out of the centre clean, then remove from oven.

Meanwhile, combine remaining cinnamon and sugar together in a small mixing bowl.

While the cakes are hot, brush tops with melted butter and sprinkle the sugar mixture over the top. Serve slices of teacake spread with butter or as a tasty warm dessert with custard.

Tip

Pecans could be used instead of walnuts. When it comes to apples, preferably use Granny Smith, as they are not too sweet and have some acidity.

IRISH PORTER CAKE (ST PATRICK'S DAY)

This recipe came from my mother who found it in A Little Irish Cookbook by John Murphy. I ate this cake a lot as a child. My mother made it often, as it was a solid cake that could be kept a long time. Now I like to make it for my family, especially on St Patrick's Day. It's a very traditional Irish fruit cake with a typical Irish twist of adding alcohol. This recipe is important to me because it celebrates my Irish roots and the need to produce good hardy food that can keep but is still fresh and delicious. The Irish always bring out a plethora of tea, cake and biscuits for visitors and this cake is a sturdy standby.

VICTORIA MCCLURG – ADELAIDE BRANCH

Preparation time: 20 minutes
Cooking time: 1½ hours
Serves: 24
Cake tin size: 25 cm round cake tin

Ingredients

375 mL bottle porter, Guinness or stout
250 g unsalted butter, chopped into cubes
1 cup brown sugar
3 cups of mixed dried fruit
3 cups plain flour
Pinch of salt
½ teaspoon bicarbonate of soda
1 teaspoon mixed spice
Grated rind of 1 small lemon
¼ cup glacé cherries (optional)
3 large free-range eggs, lightly beaten

Method

Preheat oven to 160°C (140°C fan-forced) and lightly grease a 25 cm round cake tin and line with baking paper.

Place beer, butter and sugar together in a large saucepan over a medium–low heat, stirring until butter melts. Add fruit and simmer for 10 minutes. Remove from heat and allow to cool completely.

Place cooled fruit mixture in a mixing bowl and add flour, salt, bicarbonate of soda, mixed spice, rind, cherries (if using) and whisked eggs, stirring until well combined. Spoon cake mixture into prepared tin and place on the middle shelf of preheated oven for 1¼ hours or until a skewer pushed into the centre comes out clean. Remove cake from oven and allow to cool in tin.

This cake improves with age and is best served with a cup of Irish breakfast tea.

Porter is not widely available so if using Guinness, Murphy's or other Irish stout you may wish to use 50/50 mix with water, to soften the flavour.

PLUM STREUSEL CAKE

This recipe comes from the Centenary Cookbook 1878–1978 *by St Paul's Lutheran Women, Yorketown. I have been baking this cake since the 1980s and it is a favourite with my grandchildren. In fact, most people like it, even the men in the shearing shed! When I lived in Ceduna I had a plum tree, so liked to bake this cake for friends and family when plums were in season. Now I live elsewhere friends give me plums to use. I like to take it for afternoon tea at the organisations I volunteer with.* RONDA LORIMER – KIMBA BRANCH

Method

Preheat oven to 180°C (160°C fan-forced) and lightly grease and line a 20 cm springform tin with baking paper.

For the topping, place all the ingredients together in a food processor and pulse until the mixture resembles coarse breadcrumbs. Alternatively you can place the ingredients together in a mixing bowl and rub together with fingertips until mixture resembles breadcrumbs. Set aside until required.

For the cake, place butter and sugar together in a medium mixing bowl and beat together using electric beaters until light and fluffy. Add eggs and vanilla, beating until well combined. Add flour, salt and milk, stirring until combined.

Pour cake mixture into prepared tin. Place sliced plums in a small mixing bowl with cornflour, tossing together until well coated. Gently place sliced plums over the top of the cake mixture and sprinkle over the streusel topping. Bake cake in preheated oven for 45 minutes or until a skewer comes out of the centre clean.

Serve cake warm with cream and poached plums for a decadent treat.

Tip

This cake works well with other fruit (e.g. peaches, apricots, cherries, apple or pears).

Preparation time: 20 minutes

Cooking time: 45 minutes

Serves: 8

Cake tin size: 20 cm round springform tin or 20 cm square tin

Streusel topping ingredients

60 g unsalted butter
3/4 cup caster sugar
1/4 teaspoon ground nutmeg
3/4 cup plain flour
Pinch of salt
1/4 teaspoon ground cinnamon

Cake ingredients

125 g unsalted butter
1 cup caster sugar
2 large free-range eggs, lightly beaten
1 teaspoon vanilla essence
1 1/2 cups self-raising flour
Pinch of salt
1/2 cup (125 mL) milk
350 g plums, de-stoned and sliced
1 tablespoon cornflour

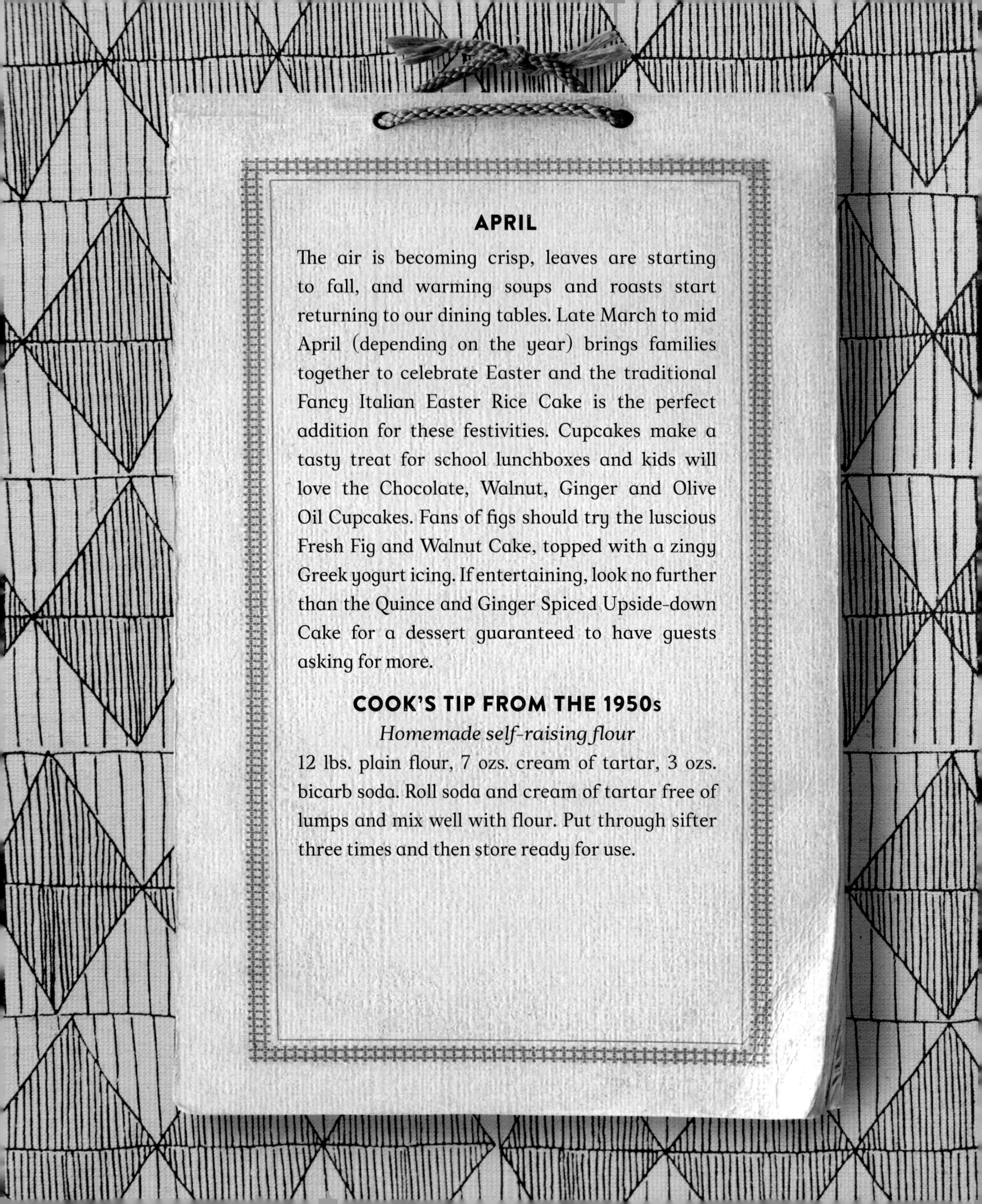

APRIL
The air is becoming crisp, leaves are starting to fall, and warming soups and roasts start returning to our dining tables. Late March to mid April (depending on the year) brings families together to celebrate Easter and the traditional Fancy Italian Easter Rice Cake is the perfect addition for these festivities. Cupcakes make a tasty treat for school lunchboxes and kids will love the Chocolate, Walnut, Ginger and Olive Oil Cupcakes. Fans of figs should try the luscious Fresh Fig and Walnut Cake, topped with a zingy Greek yogurt icing. If entertaining, look no further than the Quince and Ginger Spiced Upside-down Cake for a dessert guaranteed to have guests asking for more.
COOK'S TIP FROM THE 1950s
Homemade self-raising flour
12 lbs. plain flour, 7 ozs. cream of tartar, 3 ozs. bicarb soda. Roll soda and cream of tartar free of lumps and mix well with flour. Put through sifter three times and then store ready for use.

April

Chocolate, Walnut, Ginger and Olive Oil Cupcakes 63

Fresh Fig and Walnut Cake 64

Fancy Italian Easter Rice Cake 67

Quince and Ginger Spiced Upside-down Cake 68

CHOCOLATE, WALNUT, GINGER AND OLIVE OIL CUPCAKES

My family are olive oil producers and I have been trying out different recipes using olive oil to help promote our product and its diverse uses. I have been making this for a year and it's a family favourite. I like to make these cupcakes for the friends who help us on olive-picking days. They're very popular because of the chocolate flavour and the moistness of the cakes, thanks to the olive oil. RHONDA SEYMOUR – AUBURN BRANCH

Preparation time: 15 minutes

Cooking time: 20 minutes

Serves: 12

Cake tin size: 12-hole standard muffin pan

Ingredients

- 1¼ cup self-raising flour or gluten-free self-raising flour
- Pinch of salt
- ¼ cup cocoa
- ½ cup brown sugar
- 100 mL extra virgin olive oil or 100 g unsalted butter
- 2 large free-range eggs, lightly beaten
- ½ cup (125 mL) milk
- 1 cup chocolate chips (white, milk or dark)
- ½ cup walnuts, roughly chopped (optional)
- 1 tablespoon chopped glacé ginger (optional)

Method

Preheat oven to 180°C (160°C fan-forced) and line a 12-hole standard muffin pan with paper cases.

In a large bowl mix together flour, salt, cocoa and sugar, stirring until well combined.

Add the olive oil and eggs to a medium jug, whisking until well combined, then add to dry mixture. Partially mix using a wooden spoon, and then add milk, stirring until well combined. Add chocolate chips, walnuts and ginger, being careful not to over-stir.

Divide the mixture evenly between the paper cases and place muffin pan in preheated oven for 20 minutes or until a skewer comes out clean.

This mixture works just as well using gluten-free self-raising flour, which is readily available at most supermarkets, for anyone on a coeliac diet. Great alternatives to walnuts and ginger are slivered almonds and cranberries. Try to use Australian olive oil as it has a much better flavour and is not refined. Even better, use our Auburn olive oil.

FRESH FIG AND WALNUT CAKE

The inspiration for this cake came after a chance meeting I had with renowned South Australian chef and educator Allison Reynolds. The original recipe was developed by Allison as a banana cake for the ABC Mid North Coast 70th birthday celebrations in July 2002. I have been making it for years now. It has seriously been my 'go-to' recipe for birthdays, celebrations or I-just-need-a-cake moments. It always turns out beautifully, is super moist, and never fails to impress. I love that I could contact the original cake's creator to develop a fig version – a nod to my Greek heritage. It's such a CWA thing to do: trade and tweak recipes. TIA PSARAS – ADELAIDE BRANCH

Preparation time: 25 minutes
Cooking time: 40–45 minutes
Serves: 12
Cake tin size: 24 cm round springform pan

Ingredients

125 g unsalted butter, softened
1/4 cup brown sugar
2 large free-range eggs, lightly beaten
2 tablespoons honey
5 large fresh very ripe figs, chopped
3/4 cup Greek-style yoghurt
1 2/3 cups self-raising wholemeal flour
Pinch of salt
2 teaspoons ground cinnamon
1/4 cup of crushed walnuts
Greek yoghurt icing ingredients
1/3 cup Greek-style yoghurt
3/4 cup icing sugar, sifted
3 large firm figs, quartered

Method

Preheat oven to 180°C (160°C fan-forced) and lightly grease a round 24 cm springform tin and line the base with baking paper.

Place butter and sugar together in a large mixing bowl and beat until light and fluffy using electric beaters.

Add the eggs one at a time, beating until just combined. Add the honey, chopped fig, yoghurt, flour, salt and cinnamon and stir together with a wooden spoon until well combined.

Spoon the mixture into the prepared tin and smooth over the top leaving a slight dip in the middle of the cake mix, so that it will rise evenly.

Place tin in preheated oven and bake for 40–45 minutes or until a skewer comes out of the centre clean. Remove cake from oven and allow it to cool for 15 minutes before removing the sides of the tin. Allow to cool completely before removing base and place the cake on a platter to serve.

While the cake is cooling, combine the icing sugar and yoghurt together in a small bowl, stirring until mixture is smooth. Cover and refrigerate until the cake is cold and the icing is firm enough to spread.

To serve cake, spread icing over the top and arrange fig slices evenly around the edge.

Tip

If fresh figs are out of season, try rehydrating dried figs. Place in a bowl and just cover with boiling water. Allow to stand for several hours, or overnight (in the fridge), until the water has been absorbed. Adding too much water will dilute the flavour.

FANCY ITALIAN EASTER RICE CAKE

Every Easter my Italian mother-in-law ritualistically bakes dozens of ricotta rice cakes as Easter gifts. She uses a minimal amount of sugar but bountiful amounts of citrus, vanilla essence and a couple of cheeky shots of Italian liqueur to add colour, flavour, and a bit of edge. Growing up my father also baked a similar rice cake but with sweetened cottage cheese, spices and sultanas, which I loved! I have combined what I love about both recipes and created a variation that could be served as a fancy finale to a great Easter feast. In fact it's just not Easter in my house without the smell of this rice cake wafting through the rooms. TAMARA JAKOVLEV – ADELAIDE BRANCH

Preparation time: 30 minutes

Cooking time: 1.5 hours

Serves: 8–10

Cake tin size: 23 cm round springform tin

Cake ingredients

- 1½ litres full cream milk
- 1¼ cups white sugar
- ½ teaspoon ground cinnamon
- 1 teaspoon vanilla bean paste
- 2 lemons, peel of one and finely grated zest of the other
- 1½ cups of Arborio rice
- 5 large free-range eggs, separated
- 1 cup full fat ricotta cheese, drained of excess water
- ¾ cup of sultanas
- ¼ cup (60 mL) Galliano Vanilla Liqueur, and a cheeky 1 for you
- Finely grated zest of 1 orange
- Icing sugar, to dust

Galliano cream ingredients

- 250 g tub mascarpone cheese
- 2 tablespoons icing sugar
- 25 mL Galliano Vanilla Liqueur
- Finely grated zest of ½ an orange

Method

Preheat oven to 180°C (160°C fan-forced) and lightly grease a 23 cm round springform tin with butter and then dust with flour.

In a large saucepan bring milk, 1 cup of sugar, cinnamon, vanilla and 4 strips of lemon rind to boil over a medium heat. Reduce heat to low, add rice, cover and simmer for about 30 minutes, stirring occasionally, until liquid has been absorbed and rice mixture is creamy. Cover and allow to cool, before removing lemon rind.

Place egg whites in a large mixing bowl, and beat using electric beaters until stiff peaks form. Place the ricotta in a food processor and pulse until smooth. Add the egg yolks and remaining sugar and pulse again until well combined. Add the ricotta mixture to the cooled rice mixture, with the sultanas, Galliano and lemon and orange zest, stirring until well combined.

Add a spoonful of the beaten egg whites to the rice mixture, stirring to combine, which loosens the mixture. Gently fold the remaining egg whites into rice mixture until just combined. Pour mixture into prepared tin, bake for 1 hour or until a skewer comes out of centre clean.

Meanwhile, place mascarpone, icing sugar, Galliano and zest together in small mixing bowl, stirring to combine.

Remove cake from oven, allow to cool in tin on wire rack. Once cooled, remove cake from tin, dust with icing sugar. Serve with Galliano cream and poached pears.

Tip

Italian liqueur is optional but highly recommended, even if it doesn't make it into the cake.

QUINCE AND GINGER SPICED UPSIDE-DOWN CAKE

When I lived in the UK a work colleague introduced me to Jamaican ginger cake, which was rich and dense from the rum, with a delicious depth of flavour that reminded me of gingerbread. Being a fan of quinces, I always bottle extras for later in the year and decided to experiment by using them for an upside down cake. Knowing that ginger and quince are a match made in heaven, I created this cake and it's been a favourite dessert cake ever since. FIONA ROBERTS – ADELAIDE BRANCH

Preparation time: 15 minutes
Cooking time: 1¼ hours
Serves: 12–15
Cake tin size: 22 cm round deep springform cake tin

Ingredients

- 160 g unsalted butter
- 1 cup soft brown sugar
- 3 large free-range eggs, lightly beaten
- 1 teaspoon ground cinnamon
- 1 teaspoon ground ginger
- 1 teaspoon ground allspice
- ½ cup stem ginger, finely chopped
- 2 teaspoons finely grated lemon zest
- 2 cups self-raising flour, sifted
- Pinch of salt
- ⅓ cup (80 mL) rum
- ½ cup treacle
- ½ cup sour cream
- 400 g poached quinces (see recipe below)

Method

Preheat oven to 180°C (160°C fan-forced). Lightly grease a deep 22 cm round springform cake tin and line with baking paper.

Using an electric mixer, beat butter and sugar together until light and fluffy. Add eggs one at a time, beating until just combined.

Gently fold in cinnamon, ground ginger, allspice, stem ginger, zest, flour, salt, rum, treacle and sour cream until combined. Place poached quinces over base of prepared cake tin and pour cake mixture on top. Place tin in preheated oven, cook for 1¼ hours or until a skewer comes out of centre clean. Remove from oven, allow to cool in tin for 10 minutes before turning onto serving plate.

Serve warm with vanilla bean ice-cream or a dollop of jersey cream.

Poached quinces

Peel, halve and core 3 large quinces. Place peelings and cores in muslin bag.

Place 1 litre water, ½ cup sugar, peel of 1 orange and ¼ cup orange juice, 2 star anise and 5 mm thick slice ginger together in a large deep ovenproof saucepan over a medium heat, stirring until sugar dissolves. Add quince halves and muslin bag to the pan, adding extra water (if required) to submerge quinces. Cover with a lid and place in oven at 150°C (130°C fan-forced) for 3–4 hours. The longer quinces cook the deeper in colour they become. Remove from oven and allow to cool.

Tip

If quinces are not available, poached pears make a great substitute.

MAY

The cooler days call for robust flavours, comforting textures and cakes that beg for a second serving. Autumn is the season for slow-ripening pears, apples and fresh nuts to shine, which are showcased in the Spiced Chocolate and Pear Cake; Banana, Apple, Honey and Nut Muffins; and the Tried and True Apple Fruit Cake. This time of year provides an opportunity to celebrate the role mothers play in our lives and for children and fathers to show appreciation and gratitude. What better way to say thank you than to encourage children into the kitchen to make a Mother's Day Carrot and Pineapple Cake, finished with a crowd favourite cream-cheese frosting.

COOK'S TIP FROM THE 1950s

Easy decoration

Do this while the cake is still warm. Press an open-patterned paper d'oyley over the cake. Then cover with very fine powdered sugar and press down firmly. When d'oyley is lifted, there is a pretty lacy pattern on the cake top. Good for sponge.

May

Spiced Chocolate and Pear Cake ... 72

Mother's Day Carrot and Pineapple Cake ... 75

Banana, Apple, Honey and Nut Muffins ... 76

Tried and True Apple Fruit Cake ... 79

SPICED CHOCOLATE AND PEAR CAKE

A big, beautiful cake that cuts well and goes a long way. It's lovely for birthdays, or when there're a few people coming over. I would have made it dozens of times, but I always pull the book out and follow the recipe! I'm 82 and even though my mind and body are kept busy, I never try and guess the recipe. It doesn't matter what age you are, it's horrible to eat a cake and think 'Oh! I left the sugar out!'.

DAWN WORRALL – PARA HILLS BRANCH

Preparation time: 20 minutes

Cooking time: 50 minutes

Serves: 12

Cake tin size: 22 cm square cake tin

Cake ingredients

- 3 large free-range eggs, lightly beaten
- 1½ cups caster sugar
- 250 g unsalted butter, softened and diced
- 1 tablespoon vanilla essence
- ½ cup (125 mL) water
- 2½ cups self-raising flour
- Pinch of salt
- 2 tablespoons cocoa
- 1 teaspoon bicarbonate of soda
- 1 teaspoon ground cinnamon
- 1 teaspoon mixed spice
- 1 cup finely chopped nuts (e.g. almonds, walnuts or hazelnuts)
- 100 g chocolate bits
- 2 pears, peeled, cored and chopped into 1 cm cubes

Chocolate icing ingredients

- 2 cups icing sugar
- ¼ cup cocoa
- ½ teaspoon vanilla extract
- 1 tablespoon milk
- 75 g unsalted butter, softened and cut into cubes

Method

Preheat oven to 180°C (160°C fan-forced) and lightly grease a 22 cm square cake tin and line with baking paper.

Beat eggs, sugar, butter, vanilla and water together in the small bowl of an electric mixer on the highest speed, until light and fluffy.

Sift flour, salt, cocoa, bicarbonate of soda, cinnamon and spices together into a medium mixing bowl. Add to egg mixture and, using a wooden spoon, mix thoroughly. Add nuts, chocolate bits and pear, stirring to combine. Pour mixture into prepared pan and bake in preheated oven for 50 minutes or until skewer comes out of the centre clean. Allow cake to cool in pan for 10 minutes before turning onto a wire rack.

Meanwhile, to make the icing, combine icing sugar, cocoa, vanilla, milk and butter together in the small bowl of an electric mixer, beating until smooth.

Once the cake has cooled, spread icing over the top and serve.

A good trick for square tins is to line the tin with two sheets of paper, like a cross. Make one sheet long enough to go across and line the tin, with a little extra paper coming up above the tin on each side. Then another sheet to go the other way. It makes it easy to lift the cake out once it's cooked.

MOTHER'S DAY CARROT AND PINEAPPLE CAKE

This recipe came from a girlfriend who lived in Western Australia, in a country town called Williams (she was a member of CWA, but not sure which branch). Most carrot cake recipes call for raw grated carrots but this recipe has cooked puréed carrots, which gives it a lovely smooth consistency. This recipe is also a family favourite. BETTY FRANKLIN – COWELL BRANCH

Preparation time: 30 minutes

Cooking time: 1 hour

Serves: 8

Cake tin size: 24 cm springform pan

Cake ingredients

2 cups plain flour
Pinch of salt
2 teaspoons bicarbonate of soda
2 teaspoons ground cinnamon
2 cups sugar
1 cup (250 mL) light olive oil
3 large free-range eggs, lightly beaten
2 teaspoons vanilla essence
1½ cups cooked carrot purée (approx. 3 medium carrots)
1 cup walnut pieces, roughly chopped
1 cup desiccated coconut
¾ cup drained crushed pineapple

Candied pineapple flowers

¼ cup caster sugar
6 thin slices pineapple, peeled

Icing ingredients

125 g cream cheese, softened
45 g butter, softened
Juice of half a lemon
½ teaspoon vanilla extract
Icing sugar

Method

Preheat oven to 180°C (160°C fan-forced). Lightly grease a 24 cm round cake tin and line with baking paper.

Sift flour, salt, bicarbonate of soda and cinnamon together in a large mixing bowl. Add sugar, stirring to combine, and make a well in centre.

In a medium jug combine oil, eggs and vanilla and beat until well combined. Pour into the centre of the flour mixture, stirring until smooth.

Add carrots, walnuts, coconut and pineapple, stirring until well combined. Spoon mixture into prepared cake tin and bake in preheated oven for 1 hour or until edges leave side of tin and a skewer comes out of the centre of the cake clean. Remove from oven, leave to cool in tin for 10 minutes before turning out onto a wire rack. Turn oven down to 120°C (100°C fan-forced).

To make pineapple flowers, combine sugar and ¼ cup (60 mL) water in a small saucepan over a low heat, stirring until sugar dissolves. Increase heat to medium-high, bring to the boil and cook for 5 minutes. Brush each pineapple slice with sugar syrup and place on a wire rack over a baking tray. Bake in oven for 1 hour or until slices have dried out, but are still a little soft. Remove from oven and carefully lift off with a spatula. Gather each pineapple slice from the centre to look like a flower and place in an egg carton to cool.

To make the topping, beat cream cheese and butter together using an electric mixer until light and fluffy. Add lemon juice, vanilla and enough icing sugar to make a good spreading consistency.

Spread icing generously over cake and top with cooled pineapple flowers.

Tip

To achieve an evenly baked cake, turn it 180° halfway through cooking, in case there is a hot or cool spot in the oven.

BANANA, APPLE, HONEY AND NUT MUFFINS

I got this recipe from The New Muffin Cookbook, *by Family Circle, a book that my daughter bought for me. I have been making it for a couple of years. I like this recipe because it is okay for me to eat as a diabetic. I like to make it for CWA afternoon tea and it is well liked by the other branch members. Any apples are fine for this cake and I like to use bananas that are going black.* ANNE STUBING – WARRAMBOO BRANCH

Preparation time: 15–20 minutes

Cooking time: 20 minutes

Serves: 10–12

Cake tin size: 12-hole standard muffin tin

Ingredients

- 2 cups self-raising flour
- 1/2 cup wholemeal plain flour
- Pinch of salt
- 1 teaspoon baking powder
- 1 teaspoon ground cinnamon
- 1 teaspoon ground mixed spice
- 1 tablespoon chopped hazelnuts
- 1 tablespoon slivered almonds
- 1/3 cup honey
- 2 tablespoons olive oil
- 1 cup mashed ripe banana
- 220 g stewed apple chunks (approximately 3 peeled apples)
- 1 large free-range egg, lightly beaten
- 3/4 cup (180 mL) skim milk

Method

Preheat oven to 180°C (160°C fan-forced) and line a 12-hole standard muffin tin with paper cases.

Sift flours, salt, baking powder and spices together in a large mixing bowl. Add the hazelnuts and almonds, stirring to combine. Make a well in the centre, add the honey, oil, banana, apple, egg and milk, stirring until just combined. The batter should appear lumpy. Divide evenly between prepared muffin cases.

Bake in preheated oven for 20 minutes or until a skewer comes out of centres clean.

Tip

Don't over-mix or the muffins will be tough. A few lumps are okay.

TRIED AND TRUE APPLE FRUIT CAKE

I first made this when my husband was in hospital, over 20 years ago now. I would take it in for morning tea to share with the lovely nurses at the hospital – I've been a nurse myself and I knew they would appreciate it. It was so popular, they all wanted the recipe and within a week they had all baked it for themselves. Now I like to make it for CWA afternoon tea as it tastes lovely and is quick and easy.

MARJORIE TUCKER – CURRAMULKA BRANCH

Preparation time: 20 minutes

Cooking time: 45 minutes

Serves: 8–10

Cake tin size: 20 cm round or square

Cake ingredients

- 1½ cups self-raising flour
- Pinch of salt
- 1 cup sugar
- 1 teaspoon ground cinnamon
- 2 large free-range eggs, lightly beaten
- 125 g unsalted butter, melted and cooled
- 1 teaspoon vanilla extract
- 2 medium to large cooking apples, peeled, cored and diced into 1 cm cubes
- 1 cup sultanas, dates or other dried fruit

Topping ingredients

- ½ teaspoon ground cinnamon
- 1 tablespoon sugar

Method

Preheat oven to 180°C (160°C fan-forced) and lightly grease and line a deep 20 cm round or square cake tin with baking paper.

In a large mixing bowl mix flour, salt, sugar and cinnamon, stirring until combined. Add eggs, butter, vanilla, apple and sultanas, stirring until well combined. Spoon mixture into prepared cake tin and smooth the top.

For the topping, combine the cinnamon and sugar together in a small bowl and sprinkle over the top of the cake mixture.

Bake in preheated oven for 45 minutes or until a skewer comes out of the centre clean.

I use Granny Smith apples as they are not too sweet and have just enough acidity. I find they give the best result.

JUNE

Winter months are bliss for bakers; the warmth of the oven spreading homely aromas of baking throughout the house, enticing impatient mouths to the kitchen in the hope of a sweet reward. Citrus from the Riverland like mandarins, navel oranges, cumquats and lemons come into their own at this time of year, creating sticky, finger-licking syrup cakes, like the Little Lemon, Almond and Rosemary Cakes; Zingy Marmalade Cake; and Cumquat Cake. On cold winter nights fruit puddings drowned in custard are the perfect way to finish a meal and the Baking Dish Nashi Pear Cake makes a simple and delicious pudding served warm.

COOK'S TIP FROM THE 1950s

Creaming butter and sugar

In cold weather, add a tablespoon of boiling water when creaming butter and sugar (increase amount for large quantities). This softens the butter and helps dissolve the sugar, and also gives a better result than the method of softening the butter near the stove. Cake appears to be lighter, with finer texture.

June

Zingy Marmalade Cake 83

Cumquat Cake 84

Sticky Little Lemon, Almond and Rosemary Cakes 87

Baking Dish Nashi Pear Cake 88

ZINGY MARMALADE CAKE

Anyone who likes marmalade would like this cake. I just love the taste of it. It stays nice and fresh and it just fits the bill. My husband likes chocolate cake but he still eats this. He'll eat whatever I put in front of him! I'll make this on occasion to take to a branch meeting. We are a small branch and a happy branch, and this zingy cake is much loved. ROSE-MARIE MORRISON – HENLEY BEACH BRANCH

Method

Preheat oven to 180°C (160°C fan forced) and lightly grease a 24 cm round cake tin and line with baking paper.

Place sour cream in a large mixing bowl and gently beat with a wooden spoon until smooth. Add sugar, 3/4 cup of marmalade, lemon zest, juice and eggs, stirring until well combined. Add flour and salt, stirring gently until combined.

Spoon mixture into prepared cake tin, bake in preheated oven for 40–45 minutes or until a skewer comes out of the centre clean.

Allow cake to cool in pan for 15 minutes before turning out onto a wire rack. Heat remaining 1/2 cup marmalade with 1 tablespoon of water until mixture is runny and pour over cake while still warm.

Serve slices of cake with a dollop of thickened cream if desired.

Preparation time: 15 minutes
Cooking time: 45 minutes
Serves: 12
Cake tin size: 24 cm round cake tin

Cake ingredients

1 cup sour cream
1 cup caster sugar
1 1/4 cups chunky marmalade
Zest and juice of 1 lemon
2 large free-range eggs, lightly beaten
2 1/4 cups self-raising flour, sifted
Pinch of salt

Tip

This cake can be served warm as a dessert with whipped cream or vanilla yoghurt. Use a good quality marmalade for the best flavour.

CUMQUAT CAKE

My husband Jock and I were so proud of our cumquat tree that when we moved from our fruit block at Cadell to the retirement village at Waikerie, the tree came too. It's now the central feature of our front garden. One day when I was in the garden, a lady I didn't know stopped to ask me who owned the magnificent tree. That's how I met Ruby, who had recently moved into the village. I picked some cumquats for her and to my surprise she called on me later with a piece of this cake and the recipe. I was hooked. For cooks who have the patience to remove the many pips, their reward is a moist cake, similar to an orange cake but not as sweet with a distinctive tangy flavour. JUDITH GORDON – CADELL MORGAN BRANCH

Preparation time: 20 minutes
Cooking time: 45 minutes – 1 hour
Serves: 8
Cake tin size: 14 cm round cake tin

Cake ingredients

- 110 g whole cumquats, pips removed (mandarins can also be used)
- 2/3 cup sugar
- 140 mL vegetable oil or olive oil
- 2 large free-range eggs, lightly beaten
- 2 tablespoons milk
- 1 2/3 cups self-raising flour, sifted
- 1 teaspoon baking powder
- Candied cumquats, to decorate (optional)

Icing ingredients

- 1 tablespoon unsalted butter
- 1/4 cup cumquat or orange juice
- 3/4 cup icing sugar, sifted
- 1/2 teaspoon cumquat zest

Method

Preheat oven to 180°C (160°C fan forced) and lightly grease a 14 cm round cake tin and line with baking paper.

Place cumquats and sugar together in a food processor and blitz until mixture is smooth. Transfer cumquat mixture to a large mixing bowl.

In a large jug combine oil, eggs and milk, whisking until well combined. Add mixture to cumquat purée, with flour and baking powder, stirring until well combined.

Pour mixture into prepared cake tin and bake in preheated oven for 45 minutes to 1 hour or until a skewer comes out of the centre clean. Allow cake to cool in tin for 5 minutes before transferring to a wire rack.

For the icing, place butter and juice together in a small saucepan over a low heat until butter melts. Add icing sugar and zest, stirring until you have a smooth icing. Allow to cool slightly, before spreading over cake and topping with candied cumquats.

Tip

Water is a good substitute for milk if you run out and the cake will be lighter.

STICKY LITTLE LEMON, ALMOND AND ROSEMARY CAKES

This is not your everyday afternoon teacake. The recipe came from a family friend and I remember thinking, 'Lemon and rosemary? I'm not sure about that'. But that's the thing – you don't expect it to be good, but you taste it and you think, 'Wow!'. It's different. It's just the kind of recipe that's perfect to have with a cup of tea out in the garden. And it's heaven served with berries and cream.

SARAH FORBES QUINN – ADELAIDE BRANCH

Preparation time: 20 minutes

Cooking time: 15 minutes (mini), 30 minutes (standard) or 45 minutes (springform)

Serves: 12

Cake tin size: 24-hole mini muffin tin or 12-hole standard muffin tin or 22 cm round springform cake tin

Cake ingredients

- 1¼ cups fresh breadcrumbs
- ¾ cup almond meal
- ½ tablespoon fresh rosemary leaves, finely chopped
- 200 g golden caster sugar
- 2 teaspoons baking powder
- Zest of 1 lemon
- 200 mL olive oil
- 4 large free-range eggs, lightly beaten
- Icing sugar, to dust
- Rosemary flowers, to garnish

Lemon glaze ingredients

- Juice of 2 lemons
- ½ cup (125 mL) water
- ¼ cup golden caster sugar
- 2 sprigs rosemary

Method

Line a 24-hole mini muffin tin or 12-hole standard muffin tin with paper cases or lightly grease a 22 cm round springform cake tin and line with baking paper.

Place the breadcrumbs, almond meal, rosemary, sugar and baking powder together in a large mixing bowl, stirring until well combined. In a medium jug, whisk together lemon zest, olive oil and eggs. Pour egg mixture over the almond mixture, stirring until well combined.

Evenly divide the cake mixture between the prepared paper cases, or into the springform cake tin. Place into a cold oven. Set the oven to 180°C (160°C fan-forced) and bake for 15 minutes (mini), 30 minutes (standard) and 45 minutes (springform cake tin) or until a skewer comes out of the centre of the cakes clean.

Meanwhile to make the syrup combine juice, water, sugar and rosemary sprigs in a small saucepan over a low heat, stirring until the sugar dissolves. Increase the heat to medium, bring to a boil and cook for 5 minutes. Remove from heat and allow the rosemary to infuse.

Drizzle the syrup over the cakes while they are still warm and leave to cool.

To serve, dust cakes with icing sugar and garnish with rosemary flowers.

Tip

For a gluten-free alternative, simply substitute breadcrumbs with a gluten-free variety.

BAKING DISH NASHI PEAR CAKE

We had a property in Montacute with a couple of wood stoves – one in the kitchen and one in the laundry. In winter they warmed the house beautifully. Every weekend, family would visit, so you'd have to feed six or seven people. I'd be baking all day Friday and the kids would hang over the table and get all the pieces. Now, my son is a cook, and my son-in-law is a chef and has a cooking school. So we've all kept our hand in. MARIA OOYENDYK – KAPUNDA BRANCH

Preparation time: 30 minutes

Cooking time: 55 minutes

Serves: 6–8

Cake tin size: 25 cm x 20 cm baking tray

Topping ingredients

- 4 large nashi pears or Granny Smith apples, peeled, cored and sliced
- 3 teaspoons ground cinnamon
- ½ cup brown sugar

Cake ingredients

- 2¼ cups self-raising flour, sifted
- 4 large free-range eggs, lightly beaten
- 1½ cups caster sugar
- ⅓ cup (80 mL) orange juice
- ¾ cup (180 mL) grape seed oil, rice or maize oil
- 1 teaspoon vanilla extract

Method

Preheat oven to 180°C (160°C fan forced) and lightly grease a 25 cm x 20 cm baking dish and line with baking paper.

For the topping, place nashi pear slices, cinnamon and sugar together in a medium mixing bowl, tossing until well combined. Set aside until required.

For the cake, place flour in a large mixing bowl.

In a large jug, combine eggs, sugar, juice, oil and vanilla, beating until sugar dissolves. Add to the flour, stirring until smooth and well combined

Spoon ¾ mixture into the prepared baking dish, spread the prepared nashi pear mixture evenly over top then spoon over the remaining cake mixture. Smooth the top with a spatula.

Place baking dish in preheated oven and cook for 55 minutes or until a skewer comes out of the centre clean.

If you're not familiar with nashi pears (also known as Asian pears), they are an apple shaped fruit with a yellow pear like skin that originated in Japan. Nashi actually means pear in Japanese. They are crisp in texture like an apple, but also sweet and juicy like a pear.

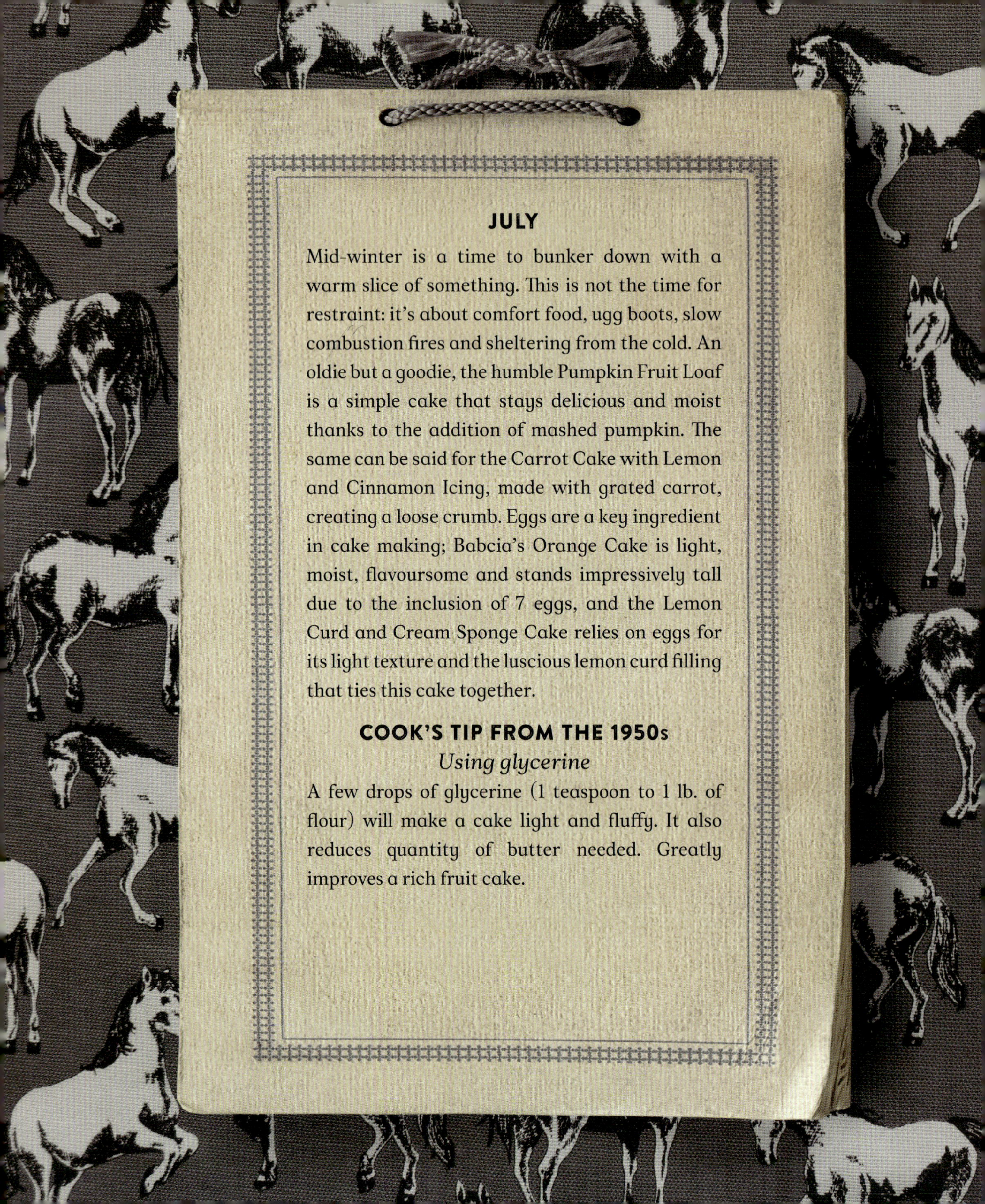

JULY

Mid-winter is a time to bunker down with a warm slice of something. This is not the time for restraint: it's about comfort food, ugg boots, slow combustion fires and sheltering from the cold. An oldie but a goodie, the humble Pumpkin Fruit Loaf is a simple cake that stays delicious and moist thanks to the addition of mashed pumpkin. The same can be said for the Carrot Cake with Lemon and Cinnamon Icing, made with grated carrot, creating a loose crumb. Eggs are a key ingredient in cake making; Babcia's Orange Cake is light, moist, flavoursome and stands impressively tall due to the inclusion of 7 eggs, and the Lemon Curd and Cream Sponge Cake relies on eggs for its light texture and the luscious lemon curd filling that ties this cake together.

COOK'S TIP FROM THE 1950s

Using glycerine

A few drops of glycerine (1 teaspoon to 1 lb. of flour) will make a cake light and fluffy. It also reduces quantity of butter needed. Greatly improves a rich fruit cake.

July

Pumpkin Fruit Loaf 92

Babcia's Orange Cake 95

Lemon Curd and Cream Sponge Cake 96

Carrot Cake with Lemon and Cinnamon Icing 99

PUMPKIN FRUIT LOAF

I had three children, but it seemed like about 14, especially at food time! As any mother with a large family, I'd make recipes out of anything I could put together. I used to make this cake for morning and afternoon teas and lunchboxes . . . if it made it that far. They'd eat it before it even got in the lunchbox!

TRENNA EATTS – MYPONGA BRANCH

Preparation time: 20 minutes
Cooking time: 1–1¼ hours
Serves: 10–12
Cake tin size: 21 cm x 12 cm x 7 cm loaf tin

Ingredients

- 115 g unsalted butter, melted
- 1 cup brown sugar
- 2 large free-range eggs, lightly beaten
- 2 tablespoons golden syrup
- 1 teaspoon vanilla extract
- 1 cup warm mashed pumpkin, strained
- 2 cups self-raising flour, sifted
- Pinch of salt
- 450 g dried mixed fruit

Method

Preheat oven to 180°C (160°C fan forced) and lightly grease and line 21 cm x 12 cm x 7 cm loaf tin with baking paper.

In a large mixing bowl, combine melted butter, sugar, eggs, golden syrup, vanilla and warmed mashed pumpkin, stirring until well combined.

Add sifted flour, salt and dried fruit, stirring until combined. Spoon mixture into prepared loaf tin and bake in preheated oven for 1–1¼ hours or until a skewer comes out of the centre clean.

Tip

Run tablespoon under hot water or spray with oil to make it easier to release golden syrup cleanly.

BABCIA'S ORANGE CAKE

This recipe was from my babcia (Polish for grandmother) and won first prize when my aunty entered it into the Royal Adelaide Show. It is the most requested of all the cakes I make. It's light, moist and full of flavour. I use homegrown oranges, when in season, otherwise I head to the markets to buy South Australian Riverland oranges as I find they are the most flavoursome. Babcia's original recipe required the rind of just one orange, but I use the rind of four; I think that's the secret to it! GEORGIA ROSS – ADELAIDE BRANCH

Preparation time: 30 minutes

Cooking time: 1 hour

Serves: 12

Cake tin size: angel cake tin

Ingredients

1½ cups of self-raising flour
Pinch of salt
1 teaspoon baking powder, heaped
7 large free-range eggs, separated
1½ cups sugar
¾ cup (180 mL) South Australian olive oil
¾ cup (180 mL) freshly squeezed orange juice
Finely grated zest of 4 oranges

Method

Preheat oven to 180°C (160°C fan forced) and lightly grease an angel cake tin with olive oil.

In a large mixing bowl sift the flour, salt and baking powder together and set aside.

In another large mixing bowl, beat egg yolks and sugar together with an electric beater until mixture becomes light and fluffy. Slowly add oil, beating until mixture becomes thick.

Slowly add the juice, rind and sifted flour mixture, stirring until well combined.

In a clean mixing bowl, beat the egg whites with electric beaters until stiff peaks form. Add a large spoonful of beaten egg whites to the flour mixture, stirring to combine, to help loosen the cake mixture. Add the remaining beaten egg whites and gently fold into the mixture, until just combined.

Pour mixture into prepared cake tin and bake in preheated oven for 1 hour or until a skewer comes out of the centre clean. Remove cake from oven and leave to cool in tin, preferably overnight.

To serve, dust cake with icing sugar or make a simple icing combining icing sugar with a little orange juice. Add flaked almonds if desired.

To add a little extra pizzazz to a simple orange icing, try adding a tablespoon of orange-flavoured liqueur, to take it to another level.

LEMON CURD AND CREAM SPONGE CAKE

Joining the Orroroo CWA branch as a new bride, members told me I should enter my citrus fruit at the Orroroo Show, urging me to 'pump-out' the septic tank onto the lemon tree occasionally (as a city chick I had no idea what a septic tank was)! After enquiring, I wondered, 'Were they having a joke with me?'. No! My massive, plump, juicy lemons stole the prize on show day. From there, members happily shared tips and recipes from their card files – lemon curd, lemon meringue, lemon pies and sponges. ILA NEIGHBOUR – SEMAPHORE BRANCH

Preparation time: 45 minutes
Cooking time: 1 hour
Serves: 8–10
Cake tin size: 20 cm deep round cake tin

Lemon curd ingredients

- 1/4 cup lemon juice
- 1/2 tablespoon finely grated lemon zest
- 2 large free-range eggs, lightly whisked and strained
- 1/2 cup caster sugar
- 65 g unsalted butter, softened

Candied lemon ingredients

- 1 cup granulated sugar
- 1 cup (250 mL) water
- Zest of 1 lemon
- 2 tablespoons caster sugar

Cake ingredients

- 4 large free-range eggs, separated
- 3/4 cup caster sugar
- 1/2 cup self-raising flour, sifted
- 1/2 cup plain flour, sifted
- Pinch of salt
- 1 teaspoon unsalted butter
- 1/3 cup (80 mL) milk
- 1 1/4 cups (310 mL) cream

Method

Preheat oven to 180°C (160°C fan forced). Lightly grease a deep 20 cm round cake tin and line with baking paper 5 cm above the top of the tin.

For lemon curd, place all the ingredients together in a non-stick saucepan over a low heat, stirring until sugar dissolves and butter melts. Keep stirring mixture continuously until curd thickens and is able to coat back of a wooden spoon, around 10–15 minutes. Once curd has thickened, allow to cool.

Meanwhile to make candied lemon peel, combine granulated sugar and water together in a small saucepan over a low heat, stirring until sugar has dissolved. Add zest, increase heat to medium and bring syrup to boil. Reduce heat and simmer for 10 minutes or until zest is translucent. Remove candied peel from syrup and allow to cool. Place caster sugar in a small bowl and add cooled candied peel, mixing until well coated.

To make cake, place egg whites in a mixing bowl and beat until soft peaks form. Gradually add sugar 1 tablespoon at a time, beating well after each addition so sugar dissolves. Add egg yolks and beat until well combined. Add sifted flours and salt and gently fold into egg mixture. Add melted butter and milk, gently fold into egg mixture. Pour cake mixture into prepared tin and bake in preheated oven for 25 minutes or until skewer comes out of centre clean. Remove from oven, allow cake to cool on wire rack.

Once cake has cooled, cut cake into 4 even layers. Spread cooled lemon curd between each layer, top cake with whipped cream and sprinkle over candied lemon zest. Refrigerate for several hours before serving.

Tip

Any leftover lemon curd can be refrigerated and used within a month.

CARROT CAKE WITH LEMON AND CINNAMON ICING

This recipe was given to me about 30 years ago and I have always enjoyed making and eating it, with or without the icing. It's been a show winner in the past at different places as we travelled around with the RAAF. The local markets around Virginia produce some of the best carrots, and I like to use locally grown sultanas and walnuts. JENNIFER DOWLING – VIRGINIA BRANCH

Preparation time: 20 minutes

Cooking time: 25 minutes for cupcakes, 1 hour for square cake

Serves: 15

Cake tin size: 20 cm square cake tin (6 cm deep)

Cake ingredients

- 3/4 cup self-raising flour
- 2/3 cup wholemeal plain flour
- Pinch of salt
- 1 teaspoon mixed spice
- 1/2 teaspoon ground cinnamon
- 1/2 teaspoon ground ginger
- 1 teaspoon bicarbonate of soda
- 3/4 cup caster sugar
- 3 large free-range eggs, whisked
- 1 cup (250 mL) olive oil
- 1 teaspoon vanilla extract
- 3/4 cup chopped walnuts
- 2 cups coarsely grated carrot
- 1/2 cup sultanas
- 1/4 cup shredded coconut
- candied carrot, to decorate

Cinnamon icing ingredients

- 1 tablespoon softened butter
- 20 g softened cream cheese
- 1/2 teaspoon vanilla extract
- Good squeeze lemon juice
- 1/4 teaspoon ground cinnamon
- 1 1/4 cups sifted icing sugar

Method

Preheat oven to 180°C (160°C fan forced). Line a 12-hole standard muffin pan with paper cases or lightly grease and line a 20 cm square cake tin with brown paper and baking paper.

In a large mixing bowl combine sifted flours, salt, spices and bicarbonate of soda Add sugar, eggs, oil, vanilla, walnuts, carrot, sultanas and coconut, stirring until well combined. Spoon mixture into prepared tin, spreading mixture into the corners. Bake in preheated oven for 25 minutes (cupcakes) or 1 hour (whole cake) or until a skewer comes out of the centre clean. Remove from oven and allow to cool in tin.

To make icing, beat butter and cream cheese in small bowl until light and fluffy. Add vanilla, juice, cinnamon and icing sugar, beating to a smooth consistency. Add extra lemon juice or icing sugar depending on the consistency you like.

Pipe or spread icing over cooled muffins or cake and top with the candied carrot.

To make candied carrot, combine 1 cup granulated sugar and 1 cup (250 mL) water together in a small saucepan over low heat, stirring until sugar has dissolved. Add 1 peeled and julienned carrot, increase heat to medium and bring syrup to the boil. Reduce heat to low, simmer for 5–10 minutes or until carrot is soft. Remove carrot from syrup and allow to cool. Place 2 tablespoons caster sugar in a small bowl, add cooled carrot, mixing until coated.

Tip

To help keep the cake moist, soak sultanas in hot water for 10 minutes to plump them up, helping to prevent them drawing moisture from the cake while it cooks.

AUGUST

All is right in the world when you have a cup of tea in hand and something sweet to savour. Aside from citrus, winter is a time to enjoy root vegetables like beetroot and potato, be it roasted, mashed, in a soup or – and this may sound bizarre – in a cake. Beetroot gives flavour and sweetness, and keeps cakes deliciously moist, partnering beautifully with chocolate, like in the decadent Chocolate, Beetroot and Almond Dessert Cake. Baking the German Streusel Spiced Potato Cake is a great way to use up left over mashed potato, giving structure, adding moistness without adding flavour, and allowing the spiced notes of nutmeg and cinnamon to shine. Olive oil is another ingredient that makes cakes deliciously soft and moist, like in the Mandarin and Olive Oil Cakes, which also use whole chopped mandarins to capture as much mandarin flavour as possible. Boozy plump sultanas folded through a plain butter mix is another way of creating a more decadent cake and is a great way of using up old sultanas.

COOK'S TIP FROM THE 1950s

Blanching almonds

Cover almonds with boiling water, and let stand a few minutes, to remove skins. Two lots of boiling water, one after the other, work very quickly. But never bring almonds to the boil in a saucepan, as this softens the nuts as well as the skins.

Boozy Southern Sultana Cake 103

German Streusel Spiced Potato Cake.....................104

Mandarin and Olive Oil Cakes 107

Chocolate, Beetroot and Almond Dessert Cake ..108

BOOZY SOUTHERN SULTANA CAKE

We used to own a hardware store and one of our workers, Mrs Tynan, would bring this cake along on special occasions. It's nice and moist and the staff members loved it. I had six children and they'd gobble it up too. Even all these years on it's still a favourite. I've kept the cake tin in the same spot in the kitchen and more often than not my adult children will sneak a piece when they come by. PAT MEYERS – ENFIELD BRANCH

Preparation time: 45 minutes

Cooking time: 1–1¼ hours

Serves: 12

Cake tin size: 1 x 23 cm cake tin or 2 x 20 cm cake tins

Ingredients

- 500 g sultanas
- 1¼ cup (310 mL) water
- ¼ cup (60 mL) sherry
- 250 g unsalted butter, softened
- 1 cup caster sugar
- 2 teaspoons cornflour
- 3 large free-range eggs, lightly beaten
- 1 cup plain flour, sifted
- 1 cup self-raising flour, sifted
- Pinch of salt
- ½ cup blanched almonds, to decorate

Method

Preheat oven to 180°C (160°C fan-forced) and lightly grease 23 cm square cake tin and line with baking paper.

Place sultanas, ¾ cup (180 mL) of water and sherry together in a medium saucepan over a low heat and slowly bring to the boil. Reduce heat and simmer until all liquid is absorbed. Remove from heat and allow to cool.

Meanwhile place butter and sugar together in the bowl of an electric mixer and beat until light and fluffy.

Place cornflour and remaining ½ cup (125 mL) cold water in a small mixing bowl, stirring until combined. Add cornflour mixture to the butter mixture, beating slowly. Add beaten eggs, one at a time, until just combined. Gradually add sifted flours and salt, stirring with a wooden spoon until just combined. Finally add the sultanas, stirring until evenly distributed.

Pour mixture into prepared cake tin, decorate top of cake with almonds and bake in preheated oven 1–1¼ hours or until a skewer comes out of the centre clean.

Tip

Use unsalted butter for baking and simply add a small pinch of salt to bring out the flavour of the cake, otherwise cake can become too salty.

GERMAN STREUSEL SPICED POTATO CAKE

My mother used to bake this as it was quick, easy and so moist and yummy. Mum made her own butter from scalded cream, which came from milk sourced from a relative's dairy. Dad grew a few potatoes (among other things) in the backyard, so it made this cake quite economical for a family treat. As a child I loved it when the cake came out of the oven and Mum turned it upside down onto the wire rack to cool, dropping bits of delicious crunchy topping into my waiting hands. BARBARA DEACY – CWA STATE OFFICE

Preparation time: 10 minutes
Cooking time: 45 minutes
Serves: 8
Cake tin size: 20 cm square or 20 cm round cake tin

Topping ingredients
- 1 cup plain flour, sifted
- 1/2 cup sugar
- 3/4 teaspoon ground cinnamon
- 1 1/2 tablespoons unsalted butter, softened

Cake ingredients
- 1/2 cup warm mashed potato
- 1 tablespoon unsalted butter
- 3/4 cup sugar
- 1 large free-range egg, lightly beaten
- 2 cups self-raising flour, sifted
- Pinch of salt
- 1 cup (250 mL) milk
- 1/2 cup sultanas
- 1 teaspoon nutmeg

Method

Preheat oven to 180°C (160°C fan-forced) and lightly grease cake tin and line with baking paper.

To make topping, combine flour, sugar, cinnamon and butter, rubbing the mixture together until it resembles breadcrumbs. Set aside for later.

In a large mixing bowl, combine warm mashed potato with butter, stirring with a wooden spoon until butter has melted. Add sugar and egg, stirring until combined. Add a little of the flour and salt, followed by a little of the milk, stirring to combine. Repeat process until all the flour and milk have been combined and the mixture is smooth.

Finally add sultanas and nutmeg, stirring until combined.

Spoon cake mixture into prepared baking tin, smoothing the top, before evenly covering with the topping mixture. Bake in preheated oven 45 minutes or until a skewer comes out of the centre clean.

Tip

If you feel like experimenting a little with this recipe, try substituting milk with buttermilk, yoghurt or sour cream, which all give slightly different textures to the cake.

MANDARIN AND OLIVE OIL CAKES

This recipe came to me from a friend who was visiting and staying with me. I have been making this cake ever since, especially when mandarins are in season or I have oranges ripe in the garden. It is simple, easy to make and always very reliable. I often make it for CWA functions, street stalls, friends and family and am continually being asked for the recipe. I have been a CWA member since I joined the Dublin branch at age 16 and have now been a member for over 60 years. I still thoroughly enjoy meetings! JEAN YOUNG – LAMEROO BRANCH

Preparation time: 12–20 minutes
Cooking time: 35 minutes
Serves: 12
Cake tin size: 1.5 litre loaf tin or 12 mini loaf tins (7 cm x 10 cm)

Ingredients

- 2 small mandarins or 1 orange, quartered and pips removed
- 2 teaspoons mandarin or orange zest
- 1 cup caster sugar
- 1¼ cups (310 mL) olive oil
- 3 large fee-range eggs, lightly beaten
- 2 cups self-raising flour, sifted

Mandarin syrup ingredients

- Zest and juice of 2 mandarins
- ½ cup sugar

Method

Preheat oven to 180°C (160°C fan-forced) and lightly grease a 1.5 litre loaf tin or 12 mini loaf tins and line with baking paper.

Place mandarin quarters (including peel) into a food processor or use a stab blender and pulse to a smooth purée.

Add zest, sugar, olive oil and eggs to the mandarin purée, pulsing until well combined. Using a spatula, scrape mixture into a medium-sized mixing bowl and add flour, stirring with a wooden spoon, until mixture is smooth.

Spoon mixture into prepared cake tin or tins. Bake in preheated oven for 20–25 minutes for mini cakes or 35 minutes for the large loaf, or until a skewer comes out of the centre clean.

Meanwhile for the syrup, combine mandarin zest, juice and sugar together in a small saucepan over a low heat, stirring until sugar dissolves. Increase heat to medium, bring to the boil and cook for 5 minutes or until mixture becomes syrupy.

Remove cake from tin or tins onto a wire rack and spoon over syrup while still hot. Allow to cool before eating.

Make sure mandarins or oranges are at room temperature before mixing.

CHOCOLATE, BEETROOT AND ALMOND DESSERT CAKE

It was always my mother's unwritten policy to make anything we ate just a little more nutritious; always halving the sugar and finding a new way to include an extra vegetable or two. In my adult life I now proudly adopt the same policy. The natural sweetness of the beetroot in this cake counters the bitterness of the dark chocolate – and I recommend going as dark as you can. BIANCA WEILER – ADELAIDE BRANCH

Preparation time: 30 minutes
Cooking time: 1 hour 15 minutes
Serves: 8
Cake tin size: 20 cm square cake tin

Cake ingredients

6 large free-range eggs, separated
½ teaspoon finely grated orange zest
2 teaspoons ground cinnamon
⅔ cup light brown sugar
225 g fresh beetroot, boiled, skins removed, cooled and finely grated
400 g dark chocolate (70% cocoa solids), roughly chopped, melted and cooled
100 mL pouring cream, whipped to soft peaks
75 g almond meal

Beetroot and orange icing ingredients

1 cup icing sugar, sifted
1 tablespoon beetroot juice
½ teaspoon orange zest

Method

Preheat oven to 180°C (160°C fan-forced). Lightly grease a 20 cm water-tight square cake tin and line with baking paper.

Using an electric mixer, whisk yolks, zest, cinnamon and two thirds of sugar for about 4 minutes or until light and fluffy. Squeeze excess juice from the grated beetroot into a bowl and set this aside to be used in the icing. Add grated beetroot and melted chocolate to the egg yolk and sugar mixture, gently folding to combine.

In a clean mixing bowl, whisk egg whites using an electric mixer until soft peaks form. Slowly add remaining sugar, a tablespoon at a time, until sugar has dissolved and mixture becomes smooth and glossy. Fold egg whites, lightly whipped cream and almond meal through chocolate mix, until just combined.

Spoon mixture into prepared cake tin. Place tin in a roasting pan and pour in enough boiling water to come halfway up the cake tin sides, creating a water bath. Bake in preheated oven for 45 minutes. Reduce oven to 150°C (130°C fan-forced) and bake for a further 30 minutes or until the cake springs back when lightly touched. Turn oven off and allow cake to cool in oven for 20 minutes. Remove from oven and allow to cool in tin.

To make icing combine icing sugar, reserved beetroot juice and zest in a small bowl, stirring until smooth.

When cake has cooled, turn onto a serving plate and drizzle with icing. If serving as a dessert, serve with thickened cream.

Tip

A good way of knowing when a cake is nearly cooked and ready to take out of the oven is to wait until you can smell it in the kitchen.

SEPTEMBER

Spring's arrival heralds new blooms and fresh scents in the air. The month kicks off with Father's Day and what better way to show your love than by treating him to a fudgy Boiled Chocolate Cake. The aspiring bakers among us are also busy baking show classics like Sponge Kisses; Gluten-free Ginger Fluff Sponges; and Jelly Cakes, for entry in the Royal Adelaide Show, where blue ribbons are hotly contested. These old-fashioned classics are all delightfully light in texture and it's practice that will perfect these little beauties. The rewards are worth it and somehow these cakes feel a little guilt free, making it very hard to stop at just one piece.

COOK'S TIP FROM THE 1950s

Brandy for fruit cakes

1. Instead of including brandy with the mixture when making fruit cake, wait until it comes cooked from the oven. Then sprinkle the brandy over the hot cake at once, where it will penetrate and give a far richer flavour.
2. Sprinkle brandy over fruit cakes before they are iced.

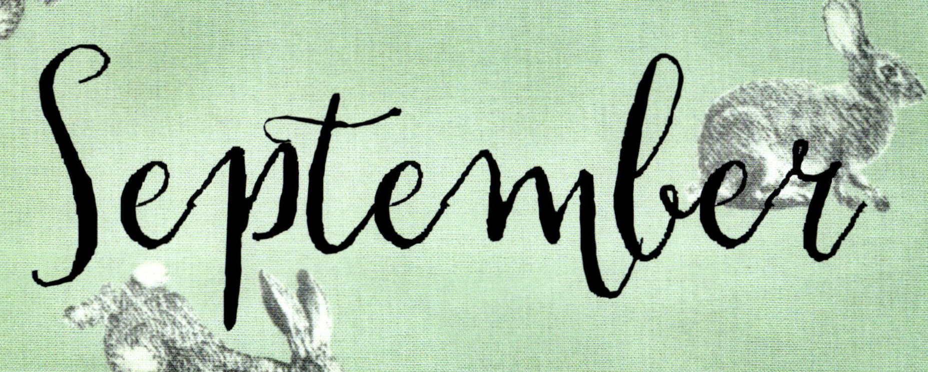

September

Father's Day Fudgy Boiled Chocolate Cake............112

Sponge Kisses............115

Gluten-free Ginger Fluff Sponge............116

Jelly Cakes............119

FATHER'S DAY FUDGY BOILED CHOCOLATE CAKE

This recipe has been handed around the family for decades – we used to make it for birthdays all the time because it makes such a big cake. My husband and I used to work at a caravan park and I would make it for the coffee shop there. One of the bus drivers would come in specifically for that chocolate cake. I'm guilty of being a bit heavy-handed with the cocoa, it makes it more chocolatey! It's one of my favourites; it's so easy to make and the end result is perfect. And everybody likes it. You can put it out anywhere and it will get eaten. HEATHER WHEELER – PENOLA BRANCH

Preparation time: 30 minutes
Cooking time: 50 minutes
Serves: 12
Cake tin size: 2 x 20 cm round deep cake tin or 1 x 28 cm round or square

Cake ingredients

2 cups (500 mL) water
3 cups caster sugar
250 g unsalted butter, chopped into small cubes
1/3 cup cocoa, sifted
1 teaspoon bicarbonate of soda
3 cups self-raising flour
Pinch of salt
4 large free-range eggs, lightly beaten

Fudge icing ingredients

90 g unsalted butter
1/3 cup (80 mL) water
1/2 cup caster sugar
1 1/2 cups icing sugar
1/3 cup cocoa, sifted

Method

Preheat oven to 180°C (160°C fan-forced) and lightly grease 2 x 20 cm deep cake tins and line with baking paper.

In a large saucepan, combine water, sugar, butter, cocoa and bicarbonate of soda together over a low heat. Stir continuously until the sugar has dissolved. Increase heat to medium, bring to boil, simmer uncovered for 5 minutes. Remove from heat and allow to cool for 10 minutes, before adding the self-raising flour, salt and eggs.

Evenly divide the chocolate mixture between the prepared cake tins and bake in preheated oven for 45 minutes for 20 cm tins and 50 minutes for 28 cm tin, or until a skewer comes out of the centre clean. Remove cakes from oven, carefully run a knife around the inside of the tins, to release the edges of the cake. Turn cakes onto wire racks to cool.

For the icing, combine butter, water and caster sugar together in a small saucepan over a medium–low heat, stirring until sugar dissolves. Sift icing sugar and cocoa into a medium-sized mixing bowl and add hot butter mixture, stirring until mixture is smooth. Cover and refrigerate until thick. Beat with a wooden spoon until mixture is spreadable.

Cut each cake in half, creating two layers. Place the bottom layer of one cake onto a serving plate. Evenly spread 1/4 of the fudge icing over the layer and place the top layer of this cake on top. Spread another 1/4 of fudge icing over the top of this layer. Repeat the process with the remaining cake, until you have a four layer cake, with four layers of fudge icing.

Tip

To prevent marking, place clean tea towel over cake before turning out onto wire rack.

SPONGE KISSES

If I don't make these at family get-togethers, my mum will. They're a family favourite and always requested. They're delicious: soft, sweet, melt in your mouth, and very hard to stop at just one! For the best results, put exactly a teaspoon on the baking tray; any more and they grow too big. And make sure to add the jam and cream at the last minute, otherwise they become mushy and soft. Because they're so light, they make the perfect afternoon tea, or after dinner, treat. MARIA ALOISI – ADELAIDE BRANCH

Preparation time: 15 minutes

Cooking time: 8 minutes

Serves: 12

Cake tin size: 2 x baking trays

Cake ingredients

- 1/4 cup plain flour
- 1/3 cup cornflour
- 1 level teaspoon cream of tartar
- 1/2 level teaspoon bicarbonate of soda
- Pinch of salt
- 2 large free-range eggs, separated
- 1/3 cup sugar

Filling ingredients

- 1/3 cup strawberry jam
- 1 cup thickened cream, whipped
- Icing sugar, to dust

Method

Preheat oven to 200°C (180°C fan-forced) and lightly grease a baking tray and line with baking paper.

Sift flours, cream of tartar, bicarbonate of soda and salt three times and set aside.

In a medium mixing bowl, beat egg whites with an electric beater until very stiff. Gradually add sugar, 1 tablespoon at a time, beating well between each addition so that sugar dissolves and mixture becomes glossy. Add yolks one at a time, beating until combined.

Gently fold the sifted flour mixture into the egg mixture, using a large metal spoon, until just combined. Place teaspoonfuls of mixture on prepared oven tray and bake in preheated oven for 8 minutes. Remove from oven and allow to cool on tray for 5 minutes, before lifting the sponges off the tray with a metal spatula onto a wire rack to cool completely.

To serve sponge kisses, pair them up to make sure the two halves are similar in size. Fill each pair with whipped cream and jam and dust with icing sugar.

Tip

To prevent the sponge kisses from getting too soft, fill them with the jam and cream two hours before serving. They can be made gluten free simply by substituting the plain flour with gluten-free plain flour.

GLUTEN-FREE GINGER FLUFF SPONGE

Over the years I've made many cakes while living on sheep and cattle stations. During this time I've made very few sponge cakes, as I've always been a little nervous of failure. But recently I decided to bite the bullet and master the sponge cake and a friend suggested I try their gluten-free ginger fluff sponge for a family birthday. It was an instant success and is set to become a family favourite. To be honest, I do not know what I was frightened of for all those years! LYNN NAGEL – BRANCH OF THE AIR

Preparation time: 20 minutes
Cooking time: 25 minutes
Serves: 12
Equipment: 2 x 20 cm springform tins

Cake ingredients

- 1 cup gluten-free corn flour (maize)
- 2 teaspoons gluten-free plain flour
- 1 teaspoon bicarbonate of soda
- 1 teaspoon cream of tartar
- 2 teaspoons ground ginger
- 1 teaspoon mixed spice
- 5 extra large free-range eggs (67g), separated
- 1/2 teaspoon vanilla essence
- 2 teaspoons treacle, warmed
- 1 cup sugar

Filling ingredients

- 1/2 cup ginger marmalade
- 1 cup thickened cream, whipped
- 1/4 cup icing sugar
- 1 tablespoon glacé ginger, chopped (optional)

Method

Preheat oven to 200°C (180°C fan-forced). Lightly grease 2 x 20 cm springform tins and line with baking paper.

Sift the flours, bicarbonate of soda, cream of tartar, ground ginger and mixed spices together 4 times and set aside.

In a small bowl combine egg yolks, vanilla and warmed treacle, stirring until well combined.

Using an electric mixer beat egg whites until stiff peaks form. While the mixer is going, add the sugar and beat for 1 minute until combined. Add the egg yolk mixture. Continue beating for 5 minutes or until sugar has dissolved and mixture has become glossy and creamy in appearance.

Carefully sift the flour mixture onto the egg mixture and fold gently using a large metal spoon, until combined. Evenly divide the mixture between the two tins using scales, to help the cake layers cook evenly.

Place tins in preheated oven and cook for 25 minutes or until centre of cakes spring back when gently touched. Remove cakes from oven, and run a knife around the inside of the tin. Turn the cakes onto wire racks to cool.

To serve, place one sponge cake on a serving plate and spread ginger marmalade over the top, followed by the whipped cream. Place the remaining cake layer on top of the cream, dust with icing sugar and sprinkle glacé ginger over the top.

Tip

Be fearless. Work quickly and lightly, sift the flour several times, and use fresh eggs.

JELLY CAKES

After my mother was married, she took a job at Anders Bakery in Glenelg. This recipe comes from her collection. I remember making these with her as a tiny girl, and I'm still making them now. They're always requested whenever I'm invited to a party; people just love them. I always use raspberry jelly, it's tradition, and the jelly has to be exactly the right consistency. These cakes have a very fine crumb and I think the secret is not to cook them as long – I cook them for 16–18 minutes – and I never use the fan. I must be doing something right – they won the Blue Ribbon at the 2013 Royal Adelaide Show.

JULIE WATT – ADELAIDE BRANCH

Preparation time: 30 minutes
Cooking time: 18 minutes
Makes: 12
Equipment: standard 12-hole muffin tray and paper cases

Ingredients

- 1 x 85 g packet raspberry jelly crystals
- 80 g unsalted butter, softened
- 1/2 cup caster sugar
- 1 teaspoon vanilla essence
- 1 large free-range egg, lightly beaten
- 1 cup self-raising flour, sifted
- Pinch of salt
- 2 tablespoons milk
- 2 cups desiccated coconut
- 1 cup thickened cream, whipped

Method

Preheat oven to 180°C (160°C fan-forced). Line a 12-hole muffin pan with paper cases. Line a tray with baking paper.

Make jelly according to pack instructions and place in fridge to cool for approximately 1¾–2 hours or until jelly is slightly thick in consistency.

Place butter, sugar and vanilla together in a large mixing bowl and, using an electric mixer, beat for approximately 10 minutes or until light and fluffy. Add egg and beat until combined. Add ½ cup flour, salt and 1 tablespoon milk, mixing until well combined, then add remaining flour and milk, again mixing until combined.

Spoon cake batter into prepared muffin pan and bake in preheated oven for 16–18 minutes, or until just golden and firm to touch. Cool slightly in the muffin pan and then transfer the cakes to a wire rack. Cool completely and remove paper cases.

When jelly is ready, remove from fridge. Place the coconut in a bowl. Dip each cake in the jelly, rolling it around until it is completely covered. Drain off excess jelly and then roll in the coconut until fully coated. Place on prepared tray. Repeat process with remaining cakes and refrigerate for 30 minutes to set.

To finish jelly cakes, tip cakes upside down to give them a flat top. Using a knife, make a slit across centre of cake almost all the way through. Fill a piping bag with whipped cream and gently pipe cream into centre of each cake.

Tip

Jelly cakes without cream refrigerate well for 1–2 days.

OCTOBER

This is the time to start pottering in the garden and planting summer vegetable patches. The reward of afternoon tea is greatly appreciated after hard work in the garden, so make merry in the kitchen, putting dried fruits to good use in cakes like the Dried Apricot Loaf and the Quandong and Walnut Cake. Quandongs are wild peaches that grow in the outback and are readily available dried online. Many people will be familiar with the German-style apple streusel cake, and the Beer and Coconut Crumble Cake also has a similar topping, but no fruit or spices; its flavour is derived from the beer. This recipe was distributed around the Port Augusta School of the Air in the 1970s, an isolated community where creativity was a necessity, due to a lack of fresh produce. A cake that is always achievable using fresh produce is the Banana and Caramel Cake. The bananas with the most flavour are the overripe ones and these can be frozen (skins off) for any time you need them.

COOK'S TIP FROM THE 1950s

Rancid butter

Rancid butter can be sweetened in two hours if immersed in cold water to which a good pinch of bicarb. soda has been added.

October

Dried Apricot Loaf 123

Beer and Coconut Crumble Cake 124

Quandong and Walnut Cake 127

Banana and Caramel Cake 128

DRIED APRICOT LOAF

I live close to the edge of the Riverland so I can access dried fruit quite easily. I've tweaked this recipe over time – it works just as well without the egg, and I have a grandson who's allergic to dairy so for him, instead of putting butter in it, I use Nuttelex. This recipe is not too sweet, it's a little bit tart. It's good for the shearers, they love it, and my husband has never been a cake eater but he eats this. It freezes very well too, so when you have unexpected visitors, you can heat it up, serve it with some custard, ice-cream or some cream, and it makes a nice dessert. MARGARET HAMPEL – LOXTON BRANCH

Preparation time: 25 minutes
Cooking time: 40 minutes
Serves: 12
Cake tin size: 20 cm round cake tin or large loaf tin

Ingredients

- 2 cups dried apricots, rinsed and chopped
- 2 cups (500 mL) water
- 200 g unsalted butter
- 2 teaspoons sugar (optional)
- 2 large free-range eggs, lightly beaten
- 2 cups self-raising flour, sifted
- Pinch of salt

Method

Preheat oven to 170°C (150°C fan-forced). Lightly grease a large loaf tin and line with baking paper.

Place apricots, water and butter together in a medium saucepan over a medium–low heat and slowly bring to the boil. Remove from heat, add the sugar, stirring until dissolved, and allow mixture to cool completely.

Add the eggs to the apricot mixture, stirring with a wooden spoon to combine. Add flour, salt and stir again until well combined. Spoon mixture into prepared loaf tin and bake in preheated oven for 40 minutes or until a skewer comes out of the centre clean. Remove from oven and allow to cool.

To serve, slice loaf and spread with butter. Store in the refrigerator.

This loaf can be frozen.

BEER AND COCONUT CRUMBLE CAKE

The recipe comes from a collection compiled by children attending the Port Augusta School of the Air in 1977, photocopied and distributed to families on the school roll. It was always a cake that was made for station hands. I would make it for lunches for the men – the recipe suggests using log tins but I made it into a large slab using a cast iron roasting dish – and they'd go through it in a day. It was quick, easy and had beer in it, which everybody liked. It's quite a high cake, with a course texture, a bit like a potato cake. It was just the thing to have with tea and coffee at smoko time, but it would make a great pudding substitute served with custard for dessert. JULIA MATERNE – KEITH BRANCH

Preparation time: 20 minutes
Cooking time: 50 minutes for slab cake or 35 minutes for each small loaf
Serves: 20
Cake tin size: 26 cm x 23 cm roasting pan or 4 small loaf tins

Topping ingredients

- 1/2 cup shredded coconut
- 1/2 cup raw sugar
- 1/2 cup plain flour, sifted
- 1/2 cup unsalted butter, cut into 1 cm cubes

Cake ingredients

- 4 cups self-raising flour
- Pinch of salt
- 2 cups raw sugar
- 125 g unsalted butter, cut into 1 cm cubes
- 3 large free-range eggs, lightly beaten
- 2 cups beer (e.g. Coopers Pale Ale)

Method

Preheat oven to 180°C (160°C fan-forced) and lightly grease a 26 cm x 23 cm roasting tin or 4 x small loaf tins and line with baking paper.

For the topping, combine coconut, sugar and flour together in a medium mixing bowl, stirring to combine. Add butter and rub into flour mixture to create a coarse crumble mixture. Set aside for later.

Put flour, salt and sugar in a food processor, pulsing to combine. Add butter and pulse until mixture resembles coarse breadcrumbs. Add eggs and beer, pulsing to combine. Spoon mixture into prepared tin and sprinkle over the topping mixture. Bake in preheated oven for 50 minutes for the slab cake and 35 minutes for the small loaf tins or until topping is golden brown and a skewer comes out of the centre clean.

Tip

Make sure beer and eggs are at room temperature before adding to cake mixture.

QUANDONG AND WALNUT CAKE

This is my own recipe out of my own head. I've been cooking for competitions since I was 13. I'm 76 now and I just love it. I don't like cooking savoury food. I'm a very plain cook, but I'll bake cakes all day long. I have a very good name in Ceduna for my baking, and I've won dozens of trophies over the years. Quandongs are so plentiful here, we get buckets of them, but you could make this cake with stewed apricots or rhubarb. I reckon any fruit you put in a cake helps keep it moist. KATH DUNN – CEDUNA BRANCH

Preparation time: 30 minutes

Cooking time: 1 hour 10 minutes

Serves: 20

Cake tin size: 22 cm square cake tin

Streusel topping ingredients

- 3/4 cup plain flour
- 1/2 cup sugar
- 1/2 cup desiccated coconut
- 1/2 teaspoon ground cinnamon
- 80 g unsalted butter, cut into 1 cm cubes

Cake ingredients

- 125 g unsalted butter, softened
- 1 cup white sugar
- 2 large free-range eggs
- 3/4 cup (180 mL) milk
- 2 cups self-raising flour, sifted
- Pinch of salt
- 1/4 cup (60 mL) quandong stewing liquid
- 1 cup stewed quandongs, cooled and drained (dried quandongs for stewing are available from Outback Pride)
- 3/4 cup walnuts, chopped

Method

Preheat oven to 180°C (160°C fan-forced). Lightly grease a 22 cm square cake tin and line with baking paper.

For the streusel topping, rub flour, sugar, coconut, cinnamon and butter together in a medium mixing bowl until mixture is crumbly. Set aside for later.

Using an electric mixer beat butter and sugar together until light and fluffy. Add eggs one at a time, beating between each addition until just combined.

Add half the milk, half the flour and salt, beating until just combined. Add remaining milk, flour and quandong stewing liquid, beating until mixture is smooth.

Add stewed quandongs and walnuts and, using a wooden spoon, stir until combined. Spoon mixture into prepared cake tin and sprinkle over the prepared streusel topping. Bake cake in preheated oven for 1 hour 10 minutes or until a skewer comes out of the centre clean. Remove from oven and allow to cool for 10 minutes in tin before turning out onto a wire rack.

Tip

I very seldom use a skewer to check if a cake is cooked. I've been taught that you put the cake to your ear. If you can hear it squealing like a kettle then it's cooked. If you can't hear any noise it's only partly cooked.

BANANA AND CARAMEL CAKE

My family were sheep farmers and wheat farmers and this recipe came off the farm. In those days we cooked in a wood stove. Cooking day was Friday and my older sisters would teach me what to do. We'd make this cake for special occasions or when we had visitors for supper. It was too good for the shearers to eat; they were rough diamonds so we would make pound cake for them and save this one for special occasions. I just remember how nice it was. It was really special in those days.

MERLE HUTTON – COWELL BRANCH

Preparation time: 20 minutes
Cooking time: 1 hour
Serves: 8–10
Cake tin size: 20 cm round cake tin or loaf tin

Cake ingredients

125 g unsalted butter
3/4 cup brown sugar
2 large free-range eggs
3 overripe bananas, peeled and mashed
1 1/2 cups self-raising flour
Pinch of salt
1 teaspoon bicarbonate of soda
3/4 cup sour cream
1 tablespoon milk

Icing ingredients

60 g unsalted butter
1/2 cup brown sugar
2 tablespoons sour cream
1 1/2 cups icing sugar, sifted

Method

Preheat oven to 180°C (160°C fan-forced). Lightly grease a 20 cm round cake tin and line with baking paper.

Using an electric mixer, beat butter and sugar together until light and fluffy. Add eggs, one at a time, mixing until just combined.

Add mashed banana, stirring with a wooden spoon until combined.

Add half of the following to the banana mixture: flour, salt, bicarbonate of soda, sour cream and milk, stirring until well combined. Add the remaining half, again stirring until well combined.

Pour mixture into prepared cake tin and bake in preheated oven for 1 hour 20 minutes, or 1 hour in a loaf tin, or until a skewer comes out of the centre clean. Remove cake from oven. Carefully run a knife around the inside of the tin, to release the edges of the cake. Turn cake onto wire rack to cool.

To make the icing, place butter and brown sugar together in a small saucepan over a low heat, stirring until melted. Add sour cream, stirring to combine. Increase heat to medium and bring to the boil, cook for 3–4 minutes or until it has caramelised. Add icing sugar, stirring until well combined.

Spread across warm cake to serve.

Tip

Peel any overripe bananas and freeze, so that you always have a good supply for making banana cakes

NOVEMBER

As the weather starts warming up gardens start coming alive, with strawberries and rhubarb in abundance (a match made in heaven), crying out to be baked in the Rhubarb and Cinnamon Teacake or as a fresh filling in the Strawberry Sponge Cake. The end of spring sees summer squashes coming into their own and the Zucchini, Cinnamon and Walnut Loaf seriously gives banana bread a run for its money. For those times when you feel like baking, then open the fridge and discover no butter or eggs – don't despair! The Date and Coffee Log Cake has only four ingredients (dates, strong hot coffee, self-raising flour and walnuts) and tastes just so good.

COOK'S TIP FROM THE 1950s

Egg substitutes

1. Sift 2 level tablespoons custard powder with the flour in any cake recipe, and beat 1 dessertspoon vinegar in with the butter and sugar. This takes the place of one egg.
2. When making a ginger or fruit cake, add 1 dessertspoon vinegar in which 1/2 teaspoon bicarb. soda has been dissolved. This replaces 2 eggs and should be added last.
3. When eggs are expensive, 1 dessertspoon vinegar added to 1 gill milk will serve the purpose of 2 eggs. The resulting cake will be quite light.

November

Zucchini, Cinnamon and Walnut Loaf 132

Rhubarb and Cinnamon Teacake 135

Date and Coffee Log 136

Strawberry Sponge Cake 139

ZUCCHINI, CINNAMON AND WALNUT LOAF

I belong to the Grange Retirement Estate and grow zucchinis in our vegetable garden. Due to the bumper crops of zucchinis I've been growing I needed to find ways to use them. I have collated and researched from all over to find different recipes using zucchinis and this is one of my favourites. There do not seem to be zucchins in the early CWA cookbooks – but there will be now! ETHEL MILL – SEMAPHORE BRANCH

Preparation time: 30 minutes
Cooking time: 45–50 minutes
Serves: 20
Cake tin size: 2 medium loaf tins

Cake ingredients

- 2 cups caster sugar
- 1/2 cup (125 mL) vegetable oil
- 3 teaspoons vanilla extract
- 3 large free-range eggs, lightly beaten
- 5 small zucchinis, grated
- 1 cup walnuts, roughly chopped
- 2 1/2 cups self-raising flour, sifted
- 1/4 teaspoon baking powder
- 2 teaspoons ground cinnamon
- 1 teaspoon salt

Method

Preheat oven to 180°C (160°C fan-forced). Lightly grease 2 medium-sized loaf tins and line with baking paper.

In a large mixing bowl add sugar, vegetable oil, vanilla and eggs, whisking until well combined. Add grated zucchini and walnuts, stirring with a wooden spoon until combined.

Sift flour, baking powder, cinnamon and salt over the zucchini mixture, stirring mixture until well combined. Evenly divide the zucchini mixture between the prepared loaf pans and bake in preheated oven for 45 minutes or until a skewer comes out of the centre of each loaf clean. Remove from oven. Allow to cool in tins for 10 minutes before turning onto a wire rack to cool.

To serve, slice zucchini loaf and spread with butter.

Tip

This loaf makes a great afternoon tea, especially when you toast the slices and serve with butter.

RHUBARB AND CINNAMON TEACAKE

I have some vigorous crowns of rhubarb growing at Newman's Nursery, and being a rhubarb devotee I just could not ignore it! This recipe was modified from an old family favourite – it was also cooked in two large bundt tins suitable for my café use. It is truly a favourite, always decadent, moist with a great texture. This recipe was also published in 2007, in my cookbook High Tea in the Garden. DIANNE HALL – ADELAIDE BRANCH

Preparation time: 15–20 minutes

Cooking time: 40–45 minutes

Serves: 8–10

Cake tin size: 24 cm round tin

Ingredients

- 125 g unsalted butter, softened
- 250 g brown sugar
- 1 teaspoon vanilla essence
- Zest of 1 lemon
- 2 large free-range eggs
- 300 g plain flour, sifted
- Pinch of salt
- 1 teaspoon bicarbonate of soda
- 1 teaspoon ground cinnamon
- 1 cup sour cream
- 475 g peeled and chopped rhubarb

Method

Preheat oven to 160°C (140°C fan-forced). Lightly grease a 24 cm round cake tin and line with baking paper.

Using an electric mixer beat butter, sugar, vanilla and zest together until light and fluffy. Add eggs one at a time, beating until just combined.

Add flour, salt, bicarbonate of soda and cinnamon, stirring with a wooden spoon until well combined.

Fold the sour cream and rhubarb into the mixture until combined. Spoon mixture into prepared cake tin and bake in preheated oven for 40–45 minutes or until a skewer comes out of the centre clean. Remove from oven and allow cake to cool in tin for 15 minutes before turning onto a wire rack.

To prevent rhubarb from sinking to the bottom of the cake tin, toss with a couple of tablespoons of flour to coat the fruit. The flour will help absorb some of the moisture and grab onto the mixture to help hold it in place.

DATE AND COFFEE LOG

A friend of mine gave this to me. It's a lovely recipe that's just about foolproof. I'm 90 and I still make it; it's just so easy. You have to like dates though, it's got so many in it! The original recipe didn't have walnuts in it but I added them in because I love them, and I make sure I always use a strong coffee, it gives it a little something. I'd sooner have a piece with a glass of sherry, but it makes a lovely afternoon teacake. MARGARET NEWELL – VICTOR HARBOR BRANCH

Preparation time: 30 minutes
Cooking time: 30 minutes
Serves: 8
Cake tin size: 7.5 cm x 25 cm log tin

Ingredients

2 cups pitted dates, chopped
1 cup strong hot coffee
1 heaped cup self-raising flour
1/2 cup chopped walnuts

Method

Preheat oven to 170°C (150°C fan-forced). Lightly grease a 7.5 cm x 25 cm log tin and line with baking paper.

Place dates in a medium mixing bowl and cover with hot coffee. Cover and leave to stand for 3 hours.

Add self-raising flour and walnuts to date mixture, stirring until well combined. Spoon mixture into prepared log tin and bake in preheated oven for 30 minutes or until a skewer comes out of the centre clean. Remove from oven and allow to cool in tin.

Slice date log and serve with butter.

Tip

To prevent cakes from becoming dry it is important not to over bake them.

STRAWBERRY SPONGE CAKE

This recipe was from Great Gran Agnes Lloyd. We remember her serving it up with her shaky hands at family occasions at her house in Gilles Plains. She taught Granny Glad, who in turn taught my mum, and when the opportunity arose for us to cook for the Saddleworth Show as kids we resurrected the recipe. That was in the 80s when everyone else was cooking fondue and flambé. If it weren't for the Saddleworth Show and Mum's encouragement I would never have learnt to bake this wonderfully light and delicious cake. I won several first and second prizes over the years for my efforts, which seemed to encourage me on as a baker to this day. GAYLE BARRY – SEVENHILL BRANCH

Preparation time: 30 minutes
Cooking time: 20 minutes
Serves: 8
Cake tin size: 2 x 20 cm round cake tins

Cake ingredients

- 4 large free-range eggs, separated
- 3 drops lemon essence
- ½ cup sugar
- ½ cup cornflour
- ¼ cup plain flour, sifted
- 1 level teaspoon cream of tartar, sifted
- 1 level teaspoon bicarbonate of soda, sifted
- Pinch of salt

Filling ingredients

- 1 cup thickened cream, whipped
- 1 punnet strawberries, hulled and sliced (reserve 2 to decorate)
- Icing sugar, to dust

Method

Preheat oven to 180°C (160°C fan-forced). Lightly grease 2 x 20 cm round cake tins and line with baking paper.

Using an electric mixer beat egg whites and lemon essence until stiff peaks form. Slowly add the sugar 1 tablespoon at a time, allowing sugar to dissolve, until mixture is thick and glossy. Add the egg yolks one at a time, beating between each addition, until combined.

Sift the cornflour, plain flour, cream of tartar, bicarbonate of soda and salt 3 times.

Carefully sift the flour mixture onto the egg mixture and fold gently using a large metal spoon, until combined. Place each cake tin on a scale, to evenly divide the mixture between the two tins, which helps the cake layers cook evenly.

Place tins in preheated oven and cook for 20 minutes or until centre of cakes spring back when gently touched. Remove cakes from oven and carefully run a knife around the inside of the tin to release the edges of the cake. Turn cakes onto wire racks to cool.

To serve, place one sponge cake on a serving plate and spread whipped cream over the top. Place sliced strawberries on top of whipped cream and place second sponge cake on top. Dust with icing sugar and decorate with remaining strawberries.

Tip

If fresh berries are not in season, this cake is equally delicious with a jar of homemade jam.

DECEMBER

Early summer is a time for festive baking; dried fruit are steeping in brandy and the house is filled with the spicy aromas of cloves, cinnamon, nutmeg, allspice and ginger, as the traditional Christmas Cake bakes slowly in the oven. If spices aren't your thing, but you love dried fruit, the Gluten-free Christmas Wreath is just for you and makes a lovely edible Christmas gift. The lead-up to Christmas is a busy time for entertaining and the Almond and Apricot Torte is guaranteed to please. On first glance it may seem strange, a cake made from crushed SAO biscuits, but rest assured this is one to try. Hot days call for cold sweet desserts and the Festive Cherry and Mixed Berry Ice-Cream Cakes are a great refreshing option for Christmas Day.

COOK'S TIP FROM THE 1950s

Good butter substitute

2 lbs. beef suet, 1 cup milk, a pinch of salt, a pinch of bicarb. soda, 2 ozs. butter. Mince suet and cook in double saucepan over boiling water for 1 hour. Strain, return to saucepan, add milk and soda, and simmer for ¾ hour. Allow to set, and then strain off any liquid. Add butter and return to saucepan until melted. Mix well as it cools, and put in basin to set. This mixture is always ready for cakes and pastry and is well worth the trouble.

December

Gluten-free Christmas Wreath 143

Good Christmas Cake 144

Festive Cherry and Mixed Berry
Ice-Cream Cakes 147

Almond and Apricot Torte 148

GLUTEN-FREE CHRISTMAS WREATH

I make two of these for the branch Christmas lunch, one for my Church Fellowship's Christmas meeting and three for my 'gluten-free' friends, as Christmas gifts, where I put candles inside the wrapping and use a disposable plate – looks fabulous! ROSALIE SMITH – PORT VINCENT BRANCH

Preparation time: 30 minutes

Cooking time: 30 minutes

Serves: 12

Equipment: 20 cm ring tin x 5 cm deep

Cake ingredients

- 3 large free-range eggs, lightly beaten
- 1 cup almond meal
- 1/2 teaspoon bicarbonate of soda
- 1 tablespoon brandy
- 2/3 cup pecan nuts, chopped
- 1/3 cup dried apricots, chopped
- 1 cup sultanas
- 1 cup raisins, chopped
- 1 cup pitted dates, chopped

Topping ingredients

- 1/4 cup diabetic apricot jam
- 12 mixed glacé cherries
- 5 glacé pineapple rings
- 12 pecan nuts

Method

Preheat oven to 180°C (160°C fan-forced) and lightly grease and line ring tin with baking paper.

In a large mixing bowl combine eggs, almond meal, bicarbonate of soda, brandy, pecans, apricots, sultanas, raisins and dates, stirring until well combined.

Spoon mixture into prepared ring tin and using some extra baking paper, press the mixture down into the tin. Place tin in preheated oven and bake for 30 minutes or until a skewer comes out of the centre clean.

Remove from oven and, while cake is still hot, turn out onto a serving plate and brush with jam. Carefully arrange the glacé fruits and pecan nuts evenly around the top of the cake. Allow to cool.

To serve, place a candle in each quarter, light and present to your guests for cutting.

Tip

Line the ring tin with non-stick baking paper. To keep the paper firm around the centre pillar secure with a rubber band. Lining tins makes it easier to remove the cake and the tin is easier to clean.

GOOD CHRISTMAS CAKE

This recipe was my mother's. She never used a recipe book, she just made cakes straight out of her head, and this one was always the best. I've always got fruit cakes in the cupboard. They keep well, they're always fresh, and if anyone comes over, it's lovely to put a piece of fruit cake on the table. I think the secret is to soak the fruit for at least two days in some port. Sometimes I soak it for a week. If it dries out, I just add more. ROSE CURTIS – MOONTA BRANCH

Preparation time: 40 minutes and soaking time

Cooking time: 2½ hours and ½ hour with oven off

Serves: 60

Equipment: 2 x 23 cm round or square cake tins, or 1 cake 20 cm round and 2 smaller cakes 1 x 16 cm round and 1 x 13 cm round

Ingredients

450 g currants
450 g sultanas
450 g raisins
1 tablespoon glacé ginger, chopped
½ cup (125 mL) brandy or port
450 g unsalted butter, softened
2 cups packed dark brown sugar
2 teaspoons ground allspice
1 teaspoon ground mace
1 teaspoon ground cinnamon
1 teaspoon ground nutmeg
2 tablespoons golden syrup
9 large free-range eggs, lightly beaten
1 heaped cup plain flour
1 heaped cup self-raising flour
Pinch of salt
1½ cups blanched almonds, to garnish

Method

Place dried fruit and brandy together in a large non-metallic mixing bowl, stirring to combine. Cover and leave to soak overnight.

Preheat oven to 200°C (180°C fan-forced) and lightly grease 2 x 23 cm cake tins or 20 cm, 16 cm and 13 cm round tins and line with a double thickness of baking paper.

Place softened butter, sugar, allspice, mace, cinnamon, nutmeg and golden syrup together in a large mixing bowl. Using electric beaters, beat the mixture until light and fluffy. Add eggs, one at a time, beating well between each addition.

Gradually add the soaked fruit, flours and salt to the butter mixture, stirring gently with a wooden spoon until well combined.

Spoon mixture into prepared cake tins and smooth the tops. Decorate the cakes with blanched almonds and place tins in preheated oven for 10 minutes, then reduce temperature to 140°C (120°C fan-forced) for 1½ hours for small cakes, and 2½ hours for 20 cm and 23 cm cakes, or until a skewer comes out of the centre of each cake clean.

Turn the oven off and leave large cakes to cool in the oven for a further 30 minutes. For the smaller cakes, remove from oven and cover with foil to cool for 30 minutes. Leave cakes to cool in tins. Remove cooled cakes from tins and peel off baking paper. Wrap in clean baking paper and foil, and keep in airtight containers until ready to eat.

Tip

All rich fruit cakes need time to 'mature' and alcohol helps them keep. Store at room temperature wrapped securely in baking paper and foil. If cake becomes a little dry, 'feed' with brandy!

FESTIVE CHERRY AND MIXED BERRY ICE-CREAM CAKES

As a young girl, I wouldn't eat Christmas pudding, so my dear mum made this for me EVERY year! Mum's version made use of her mum's old pudding mould, and the ingredients varied along with my growing tastes. We would make this together, with old Christmas records playing loudly in the background to sing along to. Cherries have always been a festive season favourite for me, with many fond memories of bowls of glistening cherries calling to me from the Christmas table! I now make these cakes ahead of time, in individual pudding moulds, for Christmas lunch or dinner. They're so easy, and I just love the fresh, local berries, perfectly in season from the Adelaide Hills! LIL SANGSTER – ADELAIDE BRANCH

Preparation time: 30 minutes

Freezing time: at least 4 hours, preferably overnight

Serves: 12

Equipment: 12 x 1/2 cup ramekin dishes or 6 x individual pudding bowls

Ingredients

- 2 litres Golden North vanilla ice-cream, softened
- 1/4 cup cherry brandy (optional)
- 1/4 teaspoon pink or red food colouring
- 250 g cherries, pitted and chopped
- 250 g strawberries, hulled and chopped
- 125 g raspberries, chopped
- 125 g blueberries
- 125 g Haigh's dessert chocolate (chocolate and orange), roughly chopped

Method

Line ramekins with enough plastic wrap to line the dish and fold back to cover the filling. This helps make it easier to remove the ice-cream cakes once frozen.

Place ice-cream, brandy, food colouring, cherries, strawberries, raspberries, blueberries and chocolate together in a large mixing bowl, stirring until well combined. Spoon mixture into prepared ramekins.

Cover the tops with the excess plastic wrap and freeze for at least 4 hours, preferably overnight.

To serve the ice-cream cakes, dip ramekins quickly into hot water. Invert onto a serving dish and remove plastic wrap. At this point, the decorating is up to you! Some options include fresh cherries, red currants, berries, melted chocolate, ice magic, or even a sprig of fresh holly.

This can also be made as one large ice-cream cake, either using a loaf pan or a pudding basin.

ALMOND AND APRICOT TORTE

Willunga is known for its almonds; they're the pride of the peninsula and this recipe shows them off so perfectly. It's not as sweet as pavlova, but it's just lovely. I've been making this for almost 40 years, and the book this recipe is written in is just about falling to pieces! JENNY HANCOCK – WILLUNGA BRANCH

Preparation time: 15 minutes

Cooking time: 20 minutes

Serves: 8–12

Equipment: 1 x 22 cm springform tin or 3 x 20 cm sandwich tins

Cake ingredients

3 large free-range egg whites
1 cup caster sugar
1 teaspoon baking powder
15 SAO biscuits, crushed
½ cup raw almonds, chopped

Topping ingredients

300mL thickened cream, whipped
2 cups fresh seasonal fruit (e.g. berries, stone fruit)

Tip

Place broken SAOs in a food processor and pulse to a coarse crumb.

Method

Preheat oven to 180°C (160°C fan-forced), lightly grease 1 x 22 cm springform tin or 3 x 20 cm sandwich tins and line with baking paper.

Using an electric mixer beat egg whites to soft peaks, until they are slightly stiff and hold their shape.

Combine caster sugar and baking powder in a small bowl. Add 1 tablespoon of sugar mixture at a time to beaten egg whites, beating after each addition until combined. The mixture will become thick and glossy.

Add crushed biscuits and chopped almonds to egg white mixture and using a large metal spoon gently fold together until just combined. Spoon the mixture into the prepared 22 cm tin and bake for 20 minutes . Remove from oven and allow to cool in tin. Once cooled, remove from tin or tins and carefully remove baking paper from the base.

To serve, top with whipped and fresh fruit, similar to a pavlova.

For an alternative, evenly divide mixture between three prepared 20 cm tins and bake in preheated oven for 12–15 minutes. Follow cooling instructions above.

For topping, place 250 g cream cheese, 1 cup icing sugar, 1 teaspoon vanilla bean paste and 2 tablespoons lemon juice together in electric mixer, beat until light, fluffy and smooth.

To serve, evenly divide ¾ cup apricot jam between the three layers. Spread cream cheese topping over two jam layers, leaving the final jam layer for cake top. Spoon a little dollop of icing onto centre of serving plate, to secure cake. Carefully place a bottom layer onto plate, followed by the second layer, finishing with jam layer top. To finish, spread cream cheese topping around edges of torte and sprinkle with ⅓ cup toasted flaked almonds. Refrigerate for at least 2 hours before serving.

CELEBRATION

Celebrations call for something special. You're creating more than just cake; it's a centrepiece, a memory, a talking point, a ritual. Whether it's intimate entertaining or something bigger, bountiful baking is the answer. Nothing is more likely to make someone smile than a homemade celebration cake, made from the heart. It can be something simple and understated like the Celebration Vanilla Cake, which is a great base for a birthday cake; or for chocolate lovers you can't beat the Chocolate Mud Cake, iced in ganache for an extra chocolate hit. If traditional fruit cake is what you identify with celebrations, look no further than Angela's Wedding Cake, which also makes a fabulous Christmas cake. For the adventurous amongst us, who also have time available, nothing beats the Pink Ombre Layer Cake. The colours can be changed to whatever you choose. This cake has serious wow factor once cut and is totally worth the effort.

COOK'S TIP FROM THE 1950s

Using cream

When using cream in place of butter in a recipe, substitute 1½ cups cream for 1 cup butter. Any milk in the recipe should be reduced by a quarter the amount (e.g. instead of 1 cup milk, use only ¾ cup).

Celebration

Angela's Wedding Cake 153

Pink Ombre Layer Cake 155

Celebration Vanilla Cake 159

Chocolate Mud Cake 160

ANGELA'S WEDDING CAKE

Every Christmas my mum, a 93-year-old member of the Mallala Branch, would help her mother make this cake. Back then, it was the most time-consuming job to take the pips out of the sultanas and raisins and wash the fruit before the cakes were made. For a family of 12 children, the end result seemed so special. My mother marvels at how easy we have it now with no seeds and no dirt in the water! We made the cake for my sister Angela's wedding 30 years ago, and I now make it to have on the roadside cuppa stops while on caravanning trips around Australia. It keeps so moist, and I love to add extra almonds for added texture and crunch. Now every Christmas I make it too, so the tradition of this cake lives on. GLENDA EVANS – DARKE PEAK BRANCH

Preparation time: 30 minutes and soaking time overnight
Cooking time: 6.5 hours
Serves: 50
Cake tin size: 28 cm round cake tin*

Cake ingredients

- 1.8 kg dried mixed fruit
- 1 cup (250 mL) water
- 1 cup (250 mL) sherry, brandy or rum
- 450 g unsalted butter
- 2 cups firmly packed dark brown sugar
- Finely grated zest of 1 lemon
- Finely grated zest of 1 orange
- 1 tablespoon treacle
- 1 teaspoon bicarbonate of soda
- 10 large free-range eggs, lightly beaten
- 3 cups plain flour, sifted
- 3/4 cup self-raising flour, sifted
- Pinch of salt
- 3/4 cup almonds (optional)

Method

In a large, deep saucepan, add dried fruit, water, sherry, butter and brown sugar over a medium–low heat, stirring until butter melts. Slowly bring mixture to the boil, stirring occasionally. Remove from heat and add zests and treacle, stirring until well combined. Add bicarbonate of soda, stirring to combine. The mixture will froth up at this point, so it's important to use a deep saucepan. Allow mixture to cool, cover and leave to stand overnight.

Preheat oven to 160°C (140°C fan-forced) and lightly grease and double line a 28 cm round cake tin with baking paper.

Add beaten eggs and sifted flours to soaked fruit mixture, stirring until well combined. Spoon mixture into prepared cake tin. Create a small crater in the centre of the cake mixture, which helps to create a flat top, while baking.

Place tin in preheated oven and bake for 30 minutes. Reduce oven temperature to 140°C (120°C fan-forced) and bake for a further 6 hours or until a skewer comes out of the centre clean.

To make the fondant icing, place the icing sugar in a large mixing bowl and create a well in the centre.

In a small saucepan, add water and gelatine together and allow mixture to sponge (swell). Place over a low heat, stirring until gelatine dissolves. Do not boil. Remove saucepan from heat, add glycerine, glucose syrup and food colouring (if using) stirring until well combined.

Fondant icing ingredients

3½ cups icing sugar sifted
1½ tablespoons cold water
2 teaspoons gelatine powder
1 tablespoon glycerine
¼ cup glucose syrup
Food colouring (optional)
½ cup apricot jam, warmed, for glaze

Pour the gelatine mixture into the centre of the icing sugar, stirring until mixture is well combined. Using clean hands knead the icing until fondant becomes smooth and pliable.

To ice cake, brush outside with apricot glaze and fill in any holes with fondant. Roll the fondant on a clean surface dusted with icing sugar, to a thickness of 3 mm. Carefully drape icing over cake, gently pushing out any air bubbles, to create a smooth surface.

NOTE

To make the wedding cake in the picture multiply the ingredient quantities by 1½ to make 1 x 28 cm, 1 x 22 cm and 1 x 13 cm cakes. For the smaller cakes bake initially for 20 minutes before reducing temperature and baking for a further 3½ hours or until a skewer comes out of the centre clean.

To make the tiered cake, cut the rounded top off the cake (if required) to create a flat surface. Place each cake upside down on a cake board slightly smaller than the cake, to hide the board once iced. Ice each cake following instructions above.

For the 22 cm and 13 cm cakes, place three skewers or cake dowel rods towards the centre in a triangle, which will support the top two tiers and trim skewers level with icing.

To assemble, position 28 cm cake in centre of cake stand and then position the 22 cm, followed by the 13 cm on top, in the centre and decorate to your liking.

Tip

To help protect the sides of the cakes from burning in the oven, wrap tins in 2 thicknesses of newspaper, with masking tape. Also, this mixture can cope with double the almonds, if desired.

PINK OMBRE LAYER CAKE

Nothing beats a good butter cake. Buttery, cakey, not too sweet – a good one is heaven. One of their most wonderful assets – apart from the cake batter tasting almost better than the end product – is that they allow you to play around with colours and flavours. I firmly believe in layering cakes too – it takes them to another level, literally and figuratively. A simple butter cake, layered, coloured carefully, then carved open to reveal different colouring is impressive. And no one but you will ever know how easy it was. MONIQUE BOWLEY – ADELAIDE BRANCH

Preparation time: 5 hours, including baking and decorating
Cooking time: 45 minutes
Serves: 15–20
Cake tin size: 3 x 20 cm round sandwich cake tins

Cake ingredients

250 g unsalted butter, softened
3/4 cup caster sugar
2 teaspoons vanilla extract
4 large free-range eggs
3 cups self-raising four, sifted
Pinch of salt
1 1/2 cups (375 mL) buttermilk
Rose pink food colouring

Buttercream icing ingredients

250 g unsalted butter, softened
2 teaspoons vanilla extract
500 g Icing sugar

Method

Preheat the oven to 170°C (150°C fan-forced). Lightly grease 3 x 20 cm round sandwich cake tins and line with baking paper.

Using an electric mixer, beat butter, sugar and vanilla together until light and fluffy.

Add the eggs, one at a time, beating between each addition until well combined.

Add half the sifted flour, salt and half the buttermilk to the egg mixture and using a large metal spoon gently fold until combined. Add the remaining flour and buttermilk and again fold into the egg mixture until combined.

Using a set of scales, divide this mixture evenly into six separate mixing bowls.

Take five bowls of cake mixture and add 2, 1, 1/2 , 1/4 , 1/8 teaspoon of rose pink food colouring accordingly, stirring each to combine. Remember you want each bowl of mixture to be slightly lighter than the one before. Please note that food colouring fades in the oven so go slightly darker.

Spoon the three darkest cake mixtures into the prepared cake tins. Bake in preheated oven for 25 minutes or until a skewer comes out of the centre clean. Remove cakes from oven, allow to cool in tins for 10 minutes before turning out onto a wire rack to cool completely.

Wash and dry cake tins, then lightly grease and line with baking paper. Spoon the remaining three bowls of cake mixture into the prepared cake tins and repeat the baking process above.

Once all cake layers have cooled, you may need to trim layers, to make them more even. Place the cakes in the freezer for 25 minutes to make it easier to cut and prevent crumbs going everywhere.

To make buttercream, beat butter and vanilla together using an electric mixer until pale and creamy. Add icing sugar in batches, beating until mixture is smooth, pale and fluffy.

To assemble cake, secure bottom layer (darkest) to a cake board or cake stand with a little of the buttercream.

Spread the sides and top with a generous amount of buttercream and sandwich the next layer on top. Repeat until all layers are iced and the lightest layer is at the top. Ice the sides and top of the cake generously with buttercream. Place in refrigerator to set the icing.

Decorate with fresh flowers (e.g. roses or poppies), bunting, cake toppers or shredded coconut.

Tip

No one ever has buttermilk in the fridge. Just add a tablespoon of lemon juice or vinegar to a cup of milk and let it sit for five minutes.

CELEBRATION VANILLA CAKE

We have chickens who provide beautiful fresh eggs regularly and I find them very useful to use in this celebration cake. I got the recipe from an Italian teacher a few years ago; it's just so lovely. It's very light, but it has a nice lemony flavour – not like sponge cakes, which can sometimes be a bit plain. It works really well every time, and I serve it dusted with icing sugar or decorated with cream and strawberries or grated chocolate. It must be cooked in an ungreased angel cake tin – which seems strange – but it's so it can be upended in the pan before taking it out. HELEN GRANT – DEQUETTEVILLE BRANCH

Preparation time: 15 minutes

Cooking time: 55 minutes

Serves: 10–12

Cake tin size: 24 cm angel cake tin or 25 cm non-stick bundt tin

Cake ingredients

7 large free-range eggs, separated
1 teaspoon cream of tartar
1 cup caster sugar
1/2 cup (125 mL) oil
1/2 cup (125 mL) orange juice
1 teaspoon vanilla essence
1 teaspoon Strega liqueur
1/2 cup self-raising flour, sifted
3 teaspoons baking powder
1 cup cornflour, sifted

Topping ingredients

1 tablespoon icing sugar
1/2 punnet fresh strawberries, hulled and quartered
or
1/4 cup jam
1 cup thickened cream, whipped

Method

Preheat oven to 180°C (160°C fan-forced). Rinse a 24 cm angel cake tin with water, tap out excess and line base of angel food cake tin with baking paper. Alternatively, lightly grease a 25 cm non-stick bundt tin.

Using an electric mixer, beat egg whites and cream of tartar together until really stiff peaks form. Spoon into bowl for later.

Using electric mixer, beat egg yolks, sugar, oil, orange juice, vanilla and Strega liqueur together until light and fluffy. Sift self-raising flour, baking powder and cornflour over egg yolk mixture and gently fold together in one direction only. Add egg whites to egg yolk mixture and again gently stir together in one direction only, until just combined.

Place in prepared tin and bake in preheated oven for 55 minutes or until a skewer comes out of deepest part clean. Remove from oven, turn cake upside down onto a lined wire rack and leave to cool for 1 hour in the tin. If tin is not a loose bottom cake pan you can turn upside down over a bottle or glass and leave to hang for at least 1 hour to cool. To release cake from pan, run a palate knife around edge of cake and turn out onto a serving plate.

To serve, place strawberries in the centre of the cake and dust with icing sugar. Alternatively, slice cake in half horizontally and spread cut surface with jam, followed by whipped cream and place top layer back on top. Dust with icing sugar.

Tip

Egg whites at room temperature gain volume and reach stiff peaks quicker.

CHOCOLATE MUD CAKE

My daughter's 21st birthday was fast approaching and a special birthday cake was needed for the celebration. She has a love of chocolate donuts and chocolate cake and the idea was formed to incorporate both. I wanted the cake to be moist, rich, and easy to bake. Out came the recipe books, as well as some intrepid internet researching. I found that combining a block of chocolate to my usual chocolate cake ingredients made for a delicious result. The cake was a hit at the party, and it will be a family favourite in any home. BARBARA WILLIAMS – COOMANDOOK BRANCH

Preparation time: 1 hour

Cooking time: 50 minutes

Serves: 15–20

Cake tin size: 24 cm round springform cake tin

Cake ingredients

1⅓ cups plain flour
Pinch of salt
2 tablespoons cocoa
1 teaspoon baking powder
½ teaspoon bicarbonate of soda
200 g good-quality dark chocolate, melted
225 g unsalted butter, softened and chopped
1 cup caster sugar
1 teaspoon vanilla extract
4 large free-range eggs
½ cup (125 mL) milk

Chocolate ganache icing ingredients

150 g dark 70% chocolate, chopped
½ cup (125 mL) cream
20 g butter

Chocolate curls

150 g milk chocolate, melted
150 g white chocolate, melted

Method

Preheat oven to 160°C (140°C fan-forced). Lightly grease a 24 cm springform cake tin and line with baking paper.

Using an electric mixer, beat butter, sugar and vanilla together until light and fluffy. Add eggs, one at a time, beating well after each addition until just combined. Add cooled melted chocolate and beat until well combined.

Sift flour, salt, cocoa, baking powder and bicarbonate of soda together into a mixing bowl.

Add ⅓ of sifted ingredients to egg mixture, followed by a ⅓ of milk, beating until well combined. Repeat process twice more, until all flour mixture and milk are incorporated and mixture is smooth.

Pour mixture into prepared tin and bake in preheated oven for 50 minutes or until skewer comes out of centre clean. Remove from oven, allow to cool in pan for 10 minutes, turn out onto wire rack to cool completely.

For chocolate ganache, combine chocolate, cream and butter together in heat proof bowl over saucepan of barely simmering water. Stir until melted and well combined. Set aside to cool to a spreadable consistency.

To make chocolate curls, spread melted milk and white chocolate, separately, 2–3 mm thick on a hard cold surface (e.g. marble). Stand at room temperature until almost set, then using a sharp knife pull towards you at an angle, creating curls. If chocolate breaks, it is set too hard.

To decorate, spread ganache over the cake, and top with chocolate curls.

Tip

A wet tea towel placed around the cake tin will help prevent cake rising in the middle.

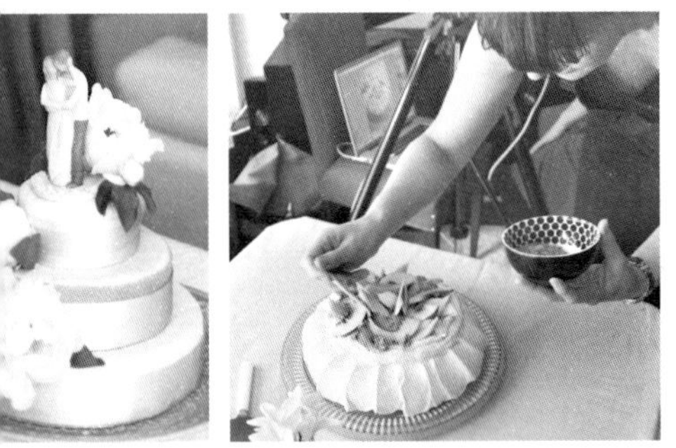

ACKNOWLEDGEMENTS

Like any cookbook, *Calendar of Cakes* has taken an enormous amount of work to co-ordinate and produce. Aside from design and publishing, this entire book has been produced by volunteers.

Firstly, a huge thank you to the visionary Julia Materne, former State President of SACWA, and Lynn Nagel, former State Treasurer of SACWA, who championed the idea of night branches to help attract younger members to the Association. Not only were these two ladies instrumental in helping get the Adelaide Branch off the ground, they embraced the idea of this cookbook and steered it through the various committees for approval. Thank you also to Linda Bertram, State President, who took over the baton from Julia and has continued the support and encouragement for this project.

With today's busy lives, it was decided a recipe a week would be far more achievable than one a day. This unfortunately meant only 52 recipes could be selected, despite receiving over 100 submissions from members across the state. I would like to thank everyone who submitted recipes; the selection process wasn't easy! Thanks to Francene Connor and Kim Adams for their assistance typing the many handwritten submissions that were selected.

Six separate photo shoots were conducted for this book, each taking a day at a time. Huge thanks to Bianca Weiler, Julie Watt, Maria Aloisi, Jenny Way, Pamela Moriarty, Georgia Ross, Lil Sangster, Monique Bowley, Margaret Porter, Tracy Smith, Nadia Rowe, Mim Gollen, Sarah Forbes-Quinn, Pat Meyers, Tia Psaras, Michelle Hornabrook, Tamara Jakovlev, Rachel Goud and Sheridan Clark who were all part of our volunteer cake-baking and recipe-testing team and whose efforts now grace the pages of this book. Thanks must also be given to our photo shoot assistants Kate Swann, Rachael Will, Claire Curry, Lil Sangster, Monique Bowley, Michelle Hornabrook, Mim Gollan, Georgia Ross, Tamara Jakovlev, Rachel Goud, Victoria McClurg and Nadia Rowe who washed dishes, weighed out ingredients, picked flowers, ironed backgrounds, shopped for last minute ingredients, made cups of tea and coffee and generally helped out. Despite all the activity in the kitchen, there was lots of chatter, cups of tea drunk and new friendships formed at these shoots, in true CWA style. Each season has a human element to help show that the CWA is for young and old. Thank you to our models Kate Swann, Pat Meyers and little Gus Rowe who all mastered the art of holding a pose, standing still and taking instruction. I would also like to thank my incredibly patient and tolerant husband for dealing with our house being turned upside down and taken over by a gaggle of girls for each shoot.

To help bring the cakes to life and add personality to these pages special thanks must be given to Nadia Rowe, Rachael Will (Vintage Carousel), Jenny and Jacqui Way, Lil Sangster and Umbrella Prints for all the amazing props and fabrics kindly loaned for each shoot.

This book is a modern twist on a community cookbook and it was important the story behind each recipe be shared with readers. A big thank to Monique Bowley, Pixie Stardust, Lisa Coyle and Lauren Gobbett for contacting contributors and collecting their stories and pictures, which add so much to the book. Thank you to Monique Bowley for editing the recipe introductions and sharing your knowledge about tools of the trade, basic preparations, cake-making methods and general baking tips in the guide to perfect baking. Thank you Pixie Stardust for researching the history of the SACWA Calendar series.

To Wakefield Press and in particular Michael Bollen, thank you for allowing this book to happen and believing in our vision. Special thanks to our fabulous editor Margot Lloyd, whose eagle eye has helped keep the manuscript consistent. A special thank you to Liz Nicholson for her beautiful design, eye for detail and ability to communicate the diverse community that is SACWA.

Finally, an enormous thank you to the very talented Jacqui Way for her tireless commitment to this project. For all the joint propping missions to our kind volunteers' shops, garages, storage cupboards and display cabinets. Thank you for chasing the daylight on those long shoots and somehow finding the last rays of light at the end, despite it looking dark to the rest of us. Thank you for helping me clean up, after the storm of each shoot, and our 9 pm Enzo dinner ritual once it was all done. In the final slog of this project, thank you for chasing all the missing pictures of contributors; it was important to represent community. Finally, thank you for creating appetite appeal and for visually making *Calendar of Cakes* the book that is.

I hope readers enjoy this book as much as the community who created it.

Happy baking!

Fiona Roberts

Food Editor

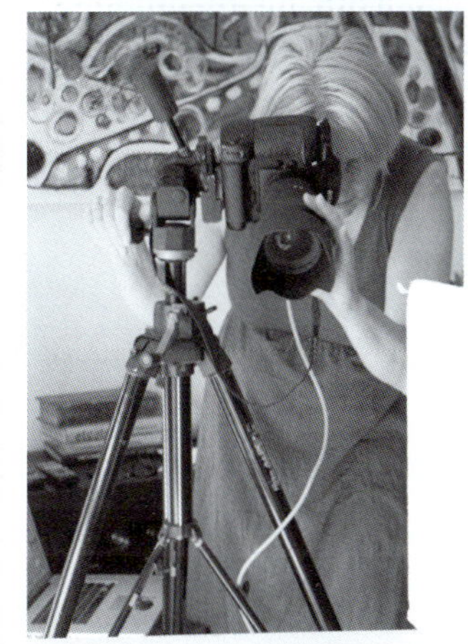

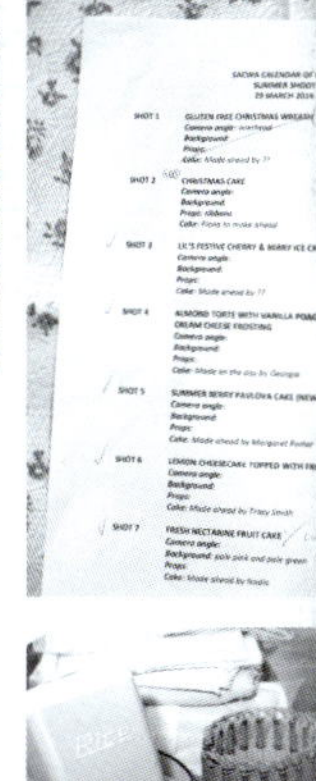

ABOUT THE CWA

The South Australian Country Women's Association has been serving the community since 1929. It is a not-for-profit, non-party political and non-sectarian organisation. The association is made up of volunteers who work to promote the welfare and conditions of life for women and children, of all ages, whether in the city or country.

The organisation's mantra is 'Sharing and Caring with Action'. Sharing involves service and the giving of time, talents, efforts and finance. What is given in service is the road to what is gained personally. Caring involves friendship, tolerance and understanding of others.

The provision of welfare is important and by working together much can be achieved. Social issues need constant monitoring and lobbying at local, state and federal levels. SACWA also believes that education is continuous, heritage skills and history are worth preserving and leisure activities enhance the quality of life.

FIONA ROBERTS – FOOD EDITOR AND STYLIST

Fiona grew up in country New South Wales, the daughter of an oyster farmer, surrounded by fresh local produce. This appreciation for country life, as well as the hard work, dedication and commitment that food producers invest to get our food from paddock to plate is at the core of Fiona's food philosophy: buy and support local, make by hand, share knowledge and skills, embrace community and educate for the future.

Fiona trained at the renowned Leiths School of Food and Wine, in London, has a Masters in Gastronomy under her belt and cut her teeth in London and Sydney's highly competitive food publishing scene, including the iconic *Australian Women's Weekly* cookbook division.

With nearly 20 years experience, internationally and locally Fiona has worked with some of the industry's most influential food writers, such as Delia Smith, Maggie Beer and Donna Hay. With a genuine interest in gastronomy, Fiona is passionate about the production of quality cookbooks that help communicate food culture at a particular time and place in history. This love of cookbooks has seen Fiona work on titles such as *Cook; Cupcakes; Cookies; Maggie's Kitchen; Simon Bryant's Vegies; Vegetables, Grains and Other Good Stuff; Korean Cookbook; Sharing Dinner Secrets;* and *Whole Foods.*

After years of living a fast-paced city life, Fiona was enticed to country South Australia to work with Maggie Beer, living in the beautiful Barossa Valley for three and a half years and consulting on new product development. Fiona now lives in Adelaide where she runs Fiona Roberts Food, a successful creative food consultancy, specialising in recipe development, food styling and food marketing.

Fiona ran the Market Kitchen program for Kids' Club and the Taste the Market cooking demonstrations at the Adelaide Showground Farmers' Market for 18 months, where she worked alongside many well-respected South Australian food producers from all over the state. It was during this time she developed a relationship with SACWA and became aware of their diminishing membership numbers. Fiona was instrumental in getting the Adelaide Branch off the ground and couldn't be happier in sharing her years of experience for this project, helping boost the SACWA brand and build future membership.

JACQUI WAY – PHOTOGRAPHER

Jacqui is an award-winning photographer who has specialised in shooting food for over 17 years. From early childhood and the influences of a country grandmother, she has had an insatiable appetite for all things edible. Her career in photography has seen her express this passion through cookbooks and magazine editorials, her clients ranging from large food companies to small local producers, restaurants and wineries.

Adding to her breadth of experience she also shoots people, fashion, lifestyle and interiors.

From cockles to chocolate, pastry and pig's bottoms, she never tires of looking for the beauty in what she photographs. Naturally the chance to shoot and eat cake with a group of lovely women for a worthy organisation was not one to pass by. She can vouch that all the cakes in this book are extremely tasty!

INDEX

Almond and Apricot Torte 148
Angela's Wedding Cake 153
Apple, Walnut and Cinnamon Teacake 55
Babcia's Orange Cake 95
Baking Dish Nashi Pear Cake 88
Banana and Caramel Cake 128
Banana, Apple, Honey and Nut Muffins 76
Beer and Coconut Crumble Cake 124
Boozy Southern Sultana Cake 103
Carrot Cake with Lemon and Cinnamon Icing 99
Celebration Vanilla Cake 159
Chocolate and Berry Roulade (Valentine's Day) 44
Chocolate, Beetroot and Almond Dessert Cake 108
Chocolate Mud Cake 160
Chocolate, Walnut, Ginger and Olive Oil Cupcakes 63
Cumquat Cake 84
Date and Coffee Log 136
Dried Apricot Loaf 123
Fancy Italian Easter Rice Cake 67
Father's Day Fudgy Boiled Chocolate Cake 112
Festive Cherry and Mixed Berry Ice-Cream Cakes 147
'Free' Blueberry and Banana Bread 43
Fresh Fig and Walnut Cake 64
German Streusel Spiced Potato Cake 104
Gluten-free Christmas Wreath 143
Gluten-free Ginger Fluff Sponge 116
Gluten-free Lamingtons (Australia Day) 39
Good Christmas Cake 144
Irish Porter Cake (St Patrick's Day) 56
Jelly Cakes 119
Lemon and Strawberry Cheesecake 35
Lemon Curd and Cream Sponge Cake 96
Mandarin and Olive Oil Cakes 107
Mother's Day Carrot and Pineapple Cake 75
Nectarine and Coconut Cupcakes 36
Peach Melba Buckle Cake 48
Pink Ombre Layer Cake 155
Plum Streusel Cake 59
Pumpkin Fruit Loaf 92
Quandong and Walnut Cake 127
Quince and Ginger Spiced Upside-down Cake 68
Raspberry Belgian Bun 47
Rhubarb and Cinnamon Teacake 135
Spiced Chocolate and Pear Cake 72
Sponge Kisses 115
Sticky Little Lemon, Almond and Rosemary Cakes 87
Strawberry Sponge Cake 139
Summer Berry Pavlova (New Year's Day) 32
Tried and True Apple Fruit Cake 79
Walnut and Fig Torte 52
Zingy Marmalade Cake 83
Zucchini, Cinnamon and Walnut Loaf 132

COUNTRY
WOMEN'S
ASSOC'N
THINKER